B Jou BIBLE

Dr. Kathleen A. Farmer, the writer of this study book, is Professor of Old Testament at United Theological Seminary, Dayton, Ohio, where she has taught since receiving her Ph.D. from Southern Methodist University in 1978. Dr. Farmer is a lay member of Fairview United Methodist Church in Dayton. She frequently teaches in adult church school classes in the Dayton area. Her publications include *Proverbs and Ecclesiastes: Who Knows What Is Good?* (Eerdmans, 1991) and "Psalms" in the *The Women's Bible Commentary,* Carol A. Newsome and Sharon H. Ringe, editors (Westminster/John Knox Press, 1992).

An official resource for The United Methodist Church prepared by the General Board of Discipleship through the division of Church School Publications and published by Cokesbury, a division of The United Methodist Publishing House; 201 Eighth Avenue, South; P. O. Box 801; Nashville, TN 37202. Printed in the United States of America. Copyright © 1994 by Cokesbury. All rights reserved.

Scripture quotations in this publication, unless otherwise indicated, are from the New Revised Standard Version of the Bible, copyright © 1989 by the Division of Christian Education of the National Council of the Churches of Christ in the United States of America, and are used by permission. All rights reserved.

For permission to reproduce any material in this publication, call 615-749-6421, or write to Cokesbury, Syndication—Permissions Office, P.O. Box 801, Nashville, TN 37202.

To order copies of this publication, call toll free 800-672-1789. Call Monday—Friday 7:30—5:00 Central Time or 8:30—4:30 Pacific Time. Use your Cokesbury account, American Express, Visa, Discover, or MasterCard.

11 12 — 19

EDITORIAL TEAM
Donn Downall,
 Editor
Norma L. Bates,
 Assistant Editor
Linda O. Spicer,
 Adult Section
 Assistant

DESIGN TEAM
Susan J. Scruggs,
 Design Supervisor,
 Cover Design
Teresa B. Travelstead,
 Designer

ADMINISTRATIVE STAFF
Neil M. Alexander,
 Vice-President,
 Publishing
Duane A. Ewers,
 Editor of Church
 School Publications
Gary L. Ball-Kilbourne,
 Executive Editor of
 Adult Publications

Cokesbury

Art Credits: pp. 4, 10, 17, 35, 46, Brenda Gilliam.

ABLE OF CONTENTS

Volume 3: Joshua, Judges, Ruth   by Kathleen Farmer

2		EDITOR'S INTRODUCTION TO THE SERIES
3		STORYTELLING IN THE OLD TESTAMENT
5	Chapter 1	FAITH TURNED INSIDE OUT
14	Chapter 2	FROM MIRACLE TO MISSION
22	Chapter 3	BY FAITH THE WALLS OF JERICHO FELL
30	Chapter 4	FROM HOMELESSNESS TO INHERITANCE
38	Chapter 5	THIS STONE SHALL BE A WITNESS
47	Chapter 6	HISTORY REPEATS ITSELF
55	Chapter 7	TURNING EXPECTATIONS UPSIDE DOWN
63	Chapter 8	TESTING: ONE, TWO, THREE
71	Chapter 9	PARENTAL DISCRETION ADVISED
80	Chapter 10	A NAZIRITE TO GOD FROM BIRTH?
87	Chapter 11	THEY DID WHAT WAS RIGHT IN THEIR OWN EYES
95	Chapter 12	LOVING-KINDNESS TRANSFORMS
103	Chapter 13	LOVING-KINDNESS GIVES BIRTH TO THE MESSIANIC LINE
111		GLOSSARY
Inside back cover		MAP OF ISRAEL IN CANAAN

$\int$ NTRODUCTION TO THE SERIES

Welcome to JOURNEY THROUGH THE BIBLE!
You are about to embark on an adventure that can change your life.

WHAT TO BRING WITH YOU

Don't worry about packing much for your trip. All you need to bring with you on this journey are
• an openness to God speaking to you in the words of Scripture
• companions to join you on the way, and
• your Bible

ITINERARY

In each session of this volume of JOURNEY THROUGH THE BIBLE, first you will be offered some hints for what to look for as you read the Bible text, and then you will be guided through four "dimensions" of study. Each is intended to help you through a well-rounded appreciation and application of the Bible's words.

HOW TO PREPARE FOR YOUR
JOURNEY THROUGH THE BIBLE

Although you will gain much if all you do is show up for Bible study and participate willingly in the session, you can do a few things to gain even more:
• Read in advance the Bible passage mentioned in What to Watch For, using the summaries and hints as you read.
• During your Bible reading, answer the questions in Dimension 1.
• Read the rest of the session in this study book.
• Try a daily discipline of reading the Bible passages suggested in Dimension 4. Note that the Bible texts listed in Dimension 4 do *not* relate to a particular session. But if you continue with this daily discipline, by the end of thirteen weeks, you will have read through *all* of that portion of the Bible covered by this volume.

Studying the Bible is a lifelong project. JOURNEY THROUGH THE BIBLE provides you with a guided tour for a few of the steps along your way. May God be with you on your journey!

Gary L. Ball-Kilbourne
Executive Editor, Adult Publications
Church School Publications

Questions or comments?
Call Curric-U-Phone 1-800-251-8591.

STORYTELLING IN THE OLD TESTAMENT

A large part of the Old Testament has been handed down to us as stories. The word *story* refers to one form in which information is presented. A story connects happenings in a sequence and reports on the speech, actions, desires, and ideas of the characters involved.

A STORY NEEDS SOMEONE TO TELL IT

The word *narrative* has basically the same meaning as *story*, but narrative is used to remind us that every story has a narrator, someone who is telling the story.

The narrator controls the amount of information the audience is given. The narrator can simply report the actions and speech of a character without judging or evaluating them. Or the narrator may draw conclusions about the characters' motives. Thus, in Joshua 2, the narrator tells us what Rahab says but makes no comment about whether her actions are right or wrong. In Joshua 9, however, the narrator says from the beginning that the Gibeonites "acted with cunning" when they came to negotiate a treaty with Israel.

Biblical stories have some distinctive features. Details are usually very sparse. Explanations of motives are few and far between. A story will almost always have several narrational gaps. Sometimes the biblical narrators are selectively and deliberately silent. We rarely hear what the narrator thinks or how the narrator feels about the actions reported.

THE NARRATOR AND YOUR IMAGINATION

The text itself never comments on the lesson to be learned from a story about Ehud, Deborah, Jael, Gideon, Jephthah, or Samson. When you read or listen to a biblical story, the narrational gaps or silences involve you in the completion of the story. The gaps allow you, invite you, even compel you to become involved. You help determine what the story means. You discover what it means to you. What you learn from reading or hearing the story depends in great part on how you close the gaps and fill in the silences in your own mind. Different readers close the gaps in different ways.

Readers sometimes assume that all the people chosen by God to carry out God's purposes must have been admirable characters. Readers who bring this assumption may try to fill in the narrative gaps with rationalizations for the characters' actions. They try to justify behavior they would normally find abhorrent. Thus, for instance, they might try to find valid reasons why Jephthah had to sacrifice his daughter. But in this study book we suggest that the stories in Joshua, Judges, and Ruth are more like mirrors than maps. They reflect the reality of human behavior, but do not map out roadways for

3

us to follow. We learn both the faithful and the unfaithful ways human beings have responded to God and to one another. Usually, it is up to the reader to judge whether the character acts in admirable ways or not.

WHAT EACH PERSON SEES OR HEARS

A single story can teach different lessons to different people. Biblical stories are always open to more than one understanding. Look at this illustration. What do you see?

Is this a picture of a chalice cup or of two faces looking at each other?

The images seem to switch back and forth. The drawing does not give enough information for the eyes to settle on either possibility. If you think of the dark area as the background and the light area as the foreground, you will see a chalice. If you think of the dark area as the foreground, then you will see two faces. Both possibilities exist within the picture itself. The same is true of biblical narratives.

SEPARATING FOREGROUND AND BACKGROUND

The understanding a reader gets from a story depends in part on what details are considered "foreground" and what are considered "background." What is more or less significant? For instance, if we focus our attention on the effect Samson's behavior has on the Philistines, we can understand Samson as a hero in the Israelites' struggle against their enemies. But if we focus on Samson's blatant disregard for Israel's covenant with God, then we understand his stories in quite a different way. Both possibilities exist within the text.

Thus, different readers can come to different conclusions about the meaning of a given story, depending on (1) how the silences in the text are filled in by the reader and (2) which details a reader considers significant or insignificant. However, not all possible readings of a biblical story are appropriate ones. Each story is found within a larger literary context (the Scriptures) that affects our understandings of that story. Each story was preserved and handed down as part of the history of the people of God. As readers we must take into account the intentions of the community of faith that handed it down.

FAITH TURNED INSIDE OUT

What to Watch For

"After the death of Moses." With those words the Book of Joshua begins.
We will discover that the transfer of authority from Moses to Joshua
changes the leaders, but does not change the people. Ahead is Israel's
actual entry into the Promised Land. Although Moses is now dead, we will
be reminded of what he has said in the past: "Know, then, that the LORD
your God is not giving you this good land to occupy because of your righteousness" (Deuteronomy 9:6). Remember as you read the first two chapters in Joshua that the men and women whose stories have been preserved
there will not always act in praiseworthy ways. We will find God choosing
to reveal God's will to human characters much like us. Each human is a
mixture of bravery and cowardice, strength and weakness, good and evil.
Expect those we meet in the Book of Joshua to be sometimes faithful,
sometimes faithless in response to God's actions and God's presence in
their lives. Joshua will add his contribution to the heritage of our faith as
he leads Israel into Canaan. So will Rahab, a Canaanite prostitute who will
be ready to help Israel to the detriment of her own people.

Read Joshua 1–2.

1. After the death of Moses, what does the LORD promise to Joshua, and what is Joshua asked to do in return? (Joshua 1:1-9)

2. What reasons does Rahab give for sheltering the two spies? (Joshua 2:8-11)

3. Read Deuteronomy 20:10-18. How carefully do the promises the two spies make to Rahab follow this command? (Joshua 2:12-14)

4. Whose actions seem to you to be the most admirable in Joshua 2? Why?

Looking Back on Failure

A connected narrative about Israel's experiences in the Promised Land continues from the beginning of the Book of Joshua through the end of Second Kings. The story starts with entrance into Canaan under the leadership of Joshua. It ends with the massive deportation known as the Babylonian Exile. In 587 B.C. the Babylonians destroyed the city of Jerusalem, burned the Temple of the LORD, and forcibly moved all the political and religious leaders of Judah into exile in Babylon.

The Story Is Gathered and Retold

While the Israelites were there in Babylon, something vital happened. The priests, the prophets, and the historians of Judah began to piece together various bits of information: oral and written translations, stories, letters, and lists. Their work led to the version of Israel's story that some scholars call the Deuteronomistic history. There had been earlier written sources. Joshua 10:13, for example, refers to the "Book of Jashar [JAY-shur]," a document that, so far as we know, is no longer in existence. Choosing what parts to use from which sources seems to have been done primarily from the perspective of the Exile, looking back. As they were writing their documents, therefore, they already knew how the story would end. Defeat and deportation were ahead in their story, for they had already happened in life. Those assembling and editing the story may have been asking themselves how an enterprise that had started out with such high hopes could have come to such a tragic end. Israel's failure to hold on to the Promised Land may have influenced which stories and which details were preserved in written form. In any case it is clear that those who handed this history down to us neither idealized their leaders nor attempted to gloss over the failures of their ancestors. These Deuteronomistic historians made it clear that God is the only hero in the history of Israel.

> Those who handed this history down to us neither idealized their leaders nor attempted to gloss over the failures of their ancestors. These Deuteronomistic historians made it clear that God is the only hero in the history of Israel.

How Will They Begin Again?

When the Babylonian Exile was brought to an end in 538 B.C., the Jews faced the prospect of returning to Jerusalem. In rebuilding both the city and the Temple, the returning exiles disagreed about who should be allowed to participate in the new community of faith. Deuteronomy had banned intermarriages between Israelites and the peoples of the land of Canaan. Ezra and Nehemiah agreed that ethnic purity was needed to ensure that the new society would remain faithful to the LORD (see Ezra 9–10 and Nehemiah 9:1-2). Ezra argued that mixed marriages had led Israelites in the past to fall into idolatrous ways. Thus he thought foreigners had to be kept out of the community of faith in order to keep worship in the new Temple pure.

The great prophet who speaks in Isaiah 56, however, insists that in this new age (after the Exile) God intends for the new Israel to be an inclusive community. According to Isaiah 56:7, it is God's will that the house of the LORD "shall be called a house of prayer for all peoples." An invitation is extended, saying that "foreigners who join themselves to the LORD" are now invited by God to become a part of the post-exilic community of faith (Isaiah 56:6). Where Deuteronomy 23:1-2 had banned those who were sexually disabled from worshiping in the Temple, Isaiah 56:3-5 heralded a new inclusiveness.

Rahab Enters the Story

The story of Rahab and the two spies might have had special significance during the period of restoration after the Exile. Persons looking for support for allowing inclusiveness in Israel could point to Rahab, an outsider by Israelites' standards because of her birth, her religion, and her manner of livelihood. But her story demonstrates that those not a part of Israel nevertheless can witness effectively to the power and presence of God.

When the leadership of Israel was transferred from Moses to Joshua, the LORD gave Joshua a task (1:6) and a series of promises. In 1:3, the language used in the promise ("I have given") indicates that the giving of the land is a completed action as far as the LORD is concerned. In 1:5, we find the LORD telling Joshua, "No one shall be able to stand against you all the days of your life." God assures him, "I will not fail you or forsake you." All that God asks of Joshua in return is strength, courage, and obedience (1:6-9). However, the story of Rahab and the spies, told just after the commissioning of Joshua, suggests that Joshua's first act of leadership is not particularly obedient or courageous.

In spite of the sweeping nature of the LORD's promises, Joshua feels the need to send out men to spy out the lay of the land. Is this simply prudence or commendable wisdom on Joshua's part? Does it show that his confidence in the sweeping promises of God is less than perfect? One clue to help us decide how to evaluate Joshua's actions is found in Joshua 2:22-24, when the spies report back to Joshua. It took a physical foray into the area around Jericho to convince both the spies and Joshua that what the LORD had said in 1:3 was true.

In contrast, Rahab, a non-Israelite and a prostitute, is able to say with complete confidence, "I know that the LORD has given you the land" (2:9). (Notice that the action in 2:8 seems completed, echoing the usage in 1:3.) Unlike the spies and Joshua, who needed the evidence of their own eyes before they believe what they had been told, Rahab is convinced by what she has heard about the power of the LORD (Joshua 2:10-11). Rahab has heard how the waters of the Red Sea were dried up for Israel's sake (Joshua 2:10). She has heard the fate of two kings who refused to let Israel pass peacefully through their territories (Numbers 21:21-35; Deuteronomy 2:26–3:7). Rahab uses the very words used in Exodus 15:15-16 to refer to the peoples upon whom "dread" will fall, or who will "melt" in fear when they hear what the LORD has done. When the spies return (verse 24) they use the same vocabulary: "All the inhabitants of the land melt in fear before us." But Rahab, the outsider, first set belief into action (Joshua 2:15-16), convinced that the LORD had given the land to Israel.

The story of Rahab has both a past and a future (as does every other story in the Bible). Words, phrases, or patterns that echo with other parts of the biblical story may give us clues to the intentions of the narrators or suggest ways the specific texts function in their larger contexts (see chart on page 10). There are a number of canonical echoes in the story of Rahab. Two relatively minor bits of information are considered together in the context of the larger story of Israel: first, Rahab is described as a prostitute (New Revised Standard Version, NRSV) or harlot (Revised Standard Version, RSV) (2:1). Second, the sending out of the spies is set geographically at Shittim [SHI-tim].

Together these minor incidents, it seems quite likely, sound a note of hope heard by the historians of Israel in the midst of their Exilic devastation. Numbers 25:1 remembers Shittim as the place where an earlier generation of Israelites "played the harlot" with the Moabite gods. (The analogy here is easier to see in the RSV than in the NRSV.) In Hebrew the same word is used to describe Rahab's occupation and the misbehavior of the Israelites at Shittim. This echo or parallel language would have been particularly significant to the Israelites in Exile; the term for "prostitution" or "harlotry" had also been used by prophets as a metaphor for Israel's dependence on foreign relationships prior to the destruction of Jerusalem. The prophets had repeatedly warned Israel that illicit liaisons with foreign nations and foreign gods would eventually bring disaster (see Isaiah 1:21; Jeremiah 3:1; Hosea 4:10, 12, 14-15; Micah 6:5). The story of Rahab, the prostitute whose faith enabled her to survive, would have echoed with hope in the ears of those who heard it retold in the midst of Exile.

> "Prostitution" had been used by prophets as a metaphor for Israel's dependence on foreign relationships prior to the destruction of Jerusalem. The prophets had repeatedly warned Israel that illicit liaisons with foreign nations would eventually bring disaster.

Echoes in the Canon

Many individual texts were gathered into the Deuteronomistic history. Beneath their surface runs a common editorial thread: confession. At least some of the Jews were ready to admit that "both we and our ancestors have sinned" (Psalm 106:6). From the perspective of the prophets, priests, and historians during the Exile, it seemed clear that God never intended to give Israel the land because of Israel's righteousness. The land had been a gift from the beginning. It was neither won nor merited. Israel had no superior power, wit, or virtue. God and God alone deserved all praise and credit for any victory. We find the same conclusion reached in the New Testament: "by grace you have been saved through faith, and this is not your own doing; it is the gift of God—not the result of works, so that no one may boast" (Ephesians 2:8-9).

God's Choices

The characters whose stories are preserved for us in Joshua are human. They are meant to be seen as mirrors of reality rather than models of morality. They are meant to reflect the people of God as they were— and as they are—not necessarily as they should be. Joshua 1:7-9 makes clear that God expects strength, courage, and obedience shown by persons chosen to perform God's will. Unfortunately, as these stories and our own life experiences tell us, God has not always received the hoped-for response (either from our ancestors or from us). The texts studied in this lesson remind us that God does not choose agents to carry out God's will on the basis of human standards of desirability.

The Rahab story reminds us that those we consider outsiders in various ways may act more faithfully and witness more effectively to God's power and presence than do insiders within the worshiping community.

At the same time, there is hope and comfort implicit in the teachings of Joshua 2. Just as Israel was promised and given the land in the midst of its lack of faith, so also does God make and keep promises to us apart from our merits. Just as God was able to use the inept spies, the prostitute, and the less-than-faithful leader to further God's purposes in the world, so also can God use us, even as we ourselves fall short of faithful actions and attitudes.

> God does not choose agents to carry out God's will on the basis of human standards of desirability. Those we consider outsiders in various ways may act more faithfully and witness more effectively to God's power and presence than do insiders within the worshiping community.

11

Is She Our Ancestor Too?

The list of the ancestors of Jesus found at the beginning of the Gospel of Matthew mentions only four women by name. Rahab is one of the four. If she is part of the lineage of the Messiah (Matthew 1:5), should we not be grateful that Holy Scripture includes her? After the destruction of Jericho, Rahab and her family become part of Israel (Joshua 6:25). Are we as Christians to give thanks that she is part of our heritage? The New Testament writers remembered Rahab in a variety of positive ways. On the one hand, the author of Hebrews includes her in the list of those who demonstrate the real nature of faith: "By faith Rahab the prostitute did not perish with those who were disobedient [or unbelieving], because she had received the spies in peace" (Hebrews 11:31). On the other hand, the author of the Book of James uses her story to support his argument that a person is *not* justified by faith alone, but that faith is completed by the works we do: "Likewise, was not Rahab the prostitute also justified by works when she welcomed the messengers and sent them out by another road?" (James 2:25).

Rahab has found her way into the New Testament three times, in Matthew 1:5, Hebrews 11:31, and James 2:25. A study of the Book of Joshua could not be considered successful without a note of thanks for Rahab.

The biblical narratives contain many examples of characters who were chosen to perform a function or who received blessings from God while their personal lives left much to be desired. Rahab was a prostitute (behavior that was clearly forbidden according to the laws of Moses). She was neither a member of God's chosen people nor a professed worshiper of the LORD. But Rahab comes across in the biblical story as a more admirable character than the men chosen by Joshua to spy out the Promised Land in the vicinity of Jericho. In fact, neither the spies nor the newly appointed leader of Israel look heroic in the first two chapters of Joshua.

Secret Agents or Bunglers?

The spies seem to bungle the job they are given: their presence in Jericho is discovered the very night they arrive. They escape with their lives only because Rahab hides them and tells lies to protect them. Should the bargain the spies make for their lives be considered an act of disobedience to the law of Moses? It is not completely clear. When the spies swear to "deal kindly" with Rahab and her family, they are at least varying from the letter of the law in Deuteronomy 20:15-18 (a deviation that Joshua will later second in 6:22-25). In any case, it is clear that when the Israelite men leave Rahab's protection they go no further on their reconnaissance mission. Instead they follow her advice and flee to the hills west of Jericho. There they hide until their pursuers get tired of looking for them. The way these details are included in the story contributes to the reader's conclusion that if the people of Jericho "melt in fear" before Israel it has to be the LORD's doing. The actions of the spies alone, as the sole representatives of the invading Israelites, would hardly have inspired fear in the hearts of the Canaanites.

Dimension 4:
A Daily Bible Journey Plan

Day 1: **Joshua 1:1-18**

Day 2: **Joshua 2:1-21**

Day 3: **Joshua 2:22–3:13**

Day 4: **Joshua 3:14–4:13**

Day 5: **Joshua 4:14-24**

Day 6: **Joshua 5:1-12**

Day 7: **Joshua 5:13–6:14**

Joshua 3–4

FROM MIRACLE TO MISSION

What to Watch For

Although it will be difficult to see when translated into English, the Hebrew root word for "crossing over" is used about twenty times in these two short chapters. We will discover powerful meaning in that idea. The story of Rahab and the spies was a brief digression away from the main thrust of the first four chapters of Joshua. Remember the beginning of Joshua 1? We were told that the LORD wanted Joshua and all the people of Israel to "proceed to cross the Jordan" (1:2). Read Joshua 3 and 4 so that you will recall how the crossing was accomplished. Keep "crossing over" in mind as a big idea.

Dimension 1: What Does the Bible Say?

1. Why were the Israelites to follow the priests who carried the ark of the covenant? How far behind it were they to stay? (Joshua 3:1-4)

2. How did the waters of the Jordan get cut off? (Joshua 3:9-17)

3. What were the twelve people representing the twelve tribes of Israel supposed to do? (Joshua 4:1-5)

4. Where were the twelve stones set up, and what purpose were they supposed to serve? (Joshua 4:6-8)

Dimension 2: What Does the Bible Mean?

It is difficult for us to follow the sequence of events described in Joshua 3 and 4. The priests carrying the ark of the covenant apparently led the way until they came to the waters of the river itself. The "cutting off" (Joshua 3:13) of the waters is said to occur as soon as the feet of the priests reach the edge of the water. But when the Israelites began to cross over, the priests apparently remained standing in the middle of the riverbed until everyone had crossed over to the Canaanite side.

Stones That Say "Remember"

Two piles of twelve stones are mentioned. One pile was apparently made of rocks taken from the middle of the Jordan. This pile was set up on the western banks of the Jordan, where the Israelites camped after they had crossed over on dry ground (4:1-7). Another pile of twelve stones was said to have been set up by Joshua in the middle of the river, where the feet of the priests had stood (4:9).

The information given in 4:19-24 seems to be mostly a duplicate of that given in 4:4-7. But these two similar passages differ about what it was Joshua wanted them to tell their children. Some Bible scholars have suggested that multiple views of this event have been preserved side by side in the present text. It is possible that the event may have been described more than once, by more than one witness. The historians of Israel may have decided to include all available accounts of such an important occasion in their history. Other scholars have suggested that the biblical text simply reflects the fact that witnesses to an exciting event often digress and backtrack as they try to tell others later what they had seen happening around them.

Surprising Geography!

Familiarity with the geographical setting is important in understanding this story. A deep crack in the crust of the earth, known as the Great Rift Valley, extends from northern Syria to central east Africa. Both the Sea of Galilee (which is actually a freshwater lake) and the Dead Sea (which has about a 25 percent salt content) lie in this deep geological fault. The Jordan River twists like a snake in the depths of the valley between these two bodies of water.

In spite of what the popular song implies, the River Jordan is neither especially deep nor wide, except in times of flood. From the Sea of Galilee southward the riverbed itself is only ninety to a hundred feet wide and from three to twelve feet deep. But when the river overflows its banks in the spring it may spread over a floodplain from 200 yards to a mile wide. The current at any time is swifter than the zigzag course of the river might indicate. The riverbed drops an average of about 9 feet a mile as its waters flow from the Sea of Galilee (about 690 feet below the level of the Mediterranean Sea) to the Dead Sea (over 1300 feet below sea level).

The Jordan valley is enclosed on both sides by steep, high hills rising as much as four thousand feet above the valley floor. The spies saved by Rahab probably hid in the steep hills that make up the canyon walls west of Jericho (Joshua 2:16, 22-23). There are three distinct levels (like natural terraces) in the Jordan valley, with as much as 150 feet difference in height between each level. The upper level is a broad tableland that receives little rain (about six inches per year). The land can be cultivated in areas where there are natural springs. The ancient city of Jericho was built around an oasis located on this upper level, about six miles west of the Jordan. The valley is about fifteen miles wide at this latitude, and the Jericho plains are nearly five hundred feet higher than the river channel. The middle level of the Rift Valley is a desolate strip of badlands, made up of bare, eroded, cone-shaped hills of greyish-white clay and gypsum. Practically nothing grows there. The lowest level of the valley is that of the floodplain of the Jordan, cut by the zigzag channel of the river itself.

River the Least of the Problems

The silt-fields of the floodplain are overgrown with a dense and nearly impenetrable thicket of tropical plants, trees, bushes, and vines. In order to reach the waters of the Jordan the Israelites would have had to (1) cross the upper terrace or tablelands, (2) climb down and across the badlands, and (3) push through the thicket or jungle of the floodplain.

The story implies that the crossing took place in the spring. The river ordinarily floods only in the spring, as the snow melts in the highlands. In the text the crossing is reported to have taken place on "the tenth day of the first month" (4:19). Modern Jewish communities celebrate the religious New Year in the autumn but most biblical passages seem to imply that the new year was at that time in the spring, at the time of the barley harvest.

The crossing of the riverbed is described as a ceremonial occasion. The Israelites march in a religious procession led by the priests who carry "the ark of the covenant of the LORD of all the earth" (3:11). The word translated "ark" refers to a portable wooden chest. Exodus 25:10-16 describes

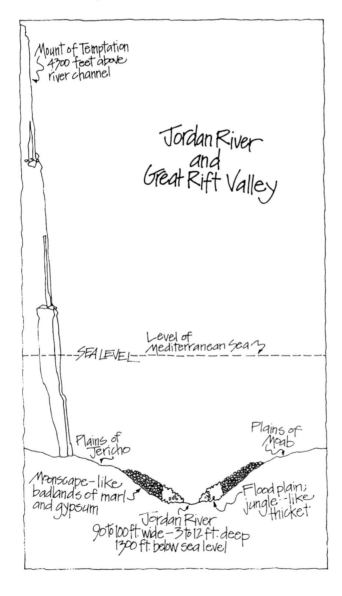

a wooden box with an overlay of gold and four rings of gold, through which poles could be inserted so it could be carried from place to place. The ark was a treasure chest of sorts. The treasure it contained was a reminder of the covenant God made with Israel at Sinai. In Deuteronomy 10:1-5, Moses says he made an "ark of acacia wood" in which to keep the two tablets of stone on which the LORD had written the Ten Commandments.

When the Ark Was There, God Was There

The ark of the covenant was ancient Israel's most sacred religious object. Notice, or count, the number of times the ark is mentioned in Joshua 3 and 4. The LORD was understood to be present whenever and wherever the ark was present. Symbolically the ark of the covenant meant it was "the LORD of all the earth" who led the Israelites to the banks of the Jordan. And the LORD's presence (symbolized by the ark) allowed the people of Israel to cross over the river on dry ground. This is one of the points made in 4:20-24. The people need to remember that it was the LORD who "dried up the waters of the Jordan."

> The LORD's presence (symbolized by the ark of the covenant) allowed the people of Israel to cross over the river on dry ground. The people need to remember that it was the LORD who "dried up the waters of the Jordan."

In addition to the many references to the ark in this section of the book, we should notice that the LORD's promise to Joshua in 1:5 ("As I was with Moses, so I will be with you") is echoed in 3:7 ("I will be with you as I was with Moses"). Thus, the presence of God with Joshua and with the people of Israel seems to be another major concern of the text. According to 3:13, the waters of the Jordan are cut off from above, not just to make the crossing easier for Israel, but so that the people will "know that among you is the living God" (3:10).

Two Crossings, the Sea and the River

The narrator seems to make a deliberate effort to draw parallels between the Jordan crossing and the Exodus story. Some of the same vocabulary is used here as in Exodus 14–15. The waters of the Jordan are said to "stand up in a single heap" (Joshua 3:13, 16) just as the waters of the sea "stood up in a heap" (Exodus 15:8). The people "cross over" on "dry ground" on both occasions (Exodus 14:22, 29; Joshua 3:17; 4:22). And both events are remembered as signs demonstrating the power of God.

Both texts use the word *fear* to describe the Israelites' response to these demonstrations of God's power. Exodus 14:31 says that when Israel saw the great work which the LORD had done, "the people feared the LORD." And Joshua 4:24 says that the waters were dried up "so that you may fear the LORD your God forever."

In the Old Testament there are instances when the presence of God seems to strike terror in the hearts of both the faithful and the unfaithful (see Exodus 20:18). Some apparently thought that seeing or hearing God directly would be overpowering enough to literally scare them to death (Exodus 33:20, 23). Others may have been afraid they would be punished for their failure to live up to God's standards (Isaiah 6:5).

But the Hebrew phrase translated "fear of the LORD" in Joshua 4:24 usually means both "understanding and behaving in God-approved ways" and "demonstrating a reverent, worshipful attitude toward God" (see Exodus 18:21). Even those who were not a part of the covenant people, even those who were strangers to the LORD, might be expected to "fear God" in this sense (see Genesis 20:11).

Dimension 3:
What Does the Bible Mean to Us?

What are the essential elements of a miracle? Biblical texts imply that an event does not have to interrupt the laws of nature (as we know them) in order for us to consider it miraculous. *Miracle* is a term that can be used to describe any extraordinary happening that people of faith believe to be the result of divine intervention.

Faith and Miracles

The eyes of faith can see God at work in the world in natural as well as in supernatural chains of cause and effect. There have been attempts to explain how the drying up of the waters in both Exodus and in Joshua might have occurred naturally (according to the laws of nature).

The Jordan rift valley is subject to massive earthquakes. There have been occasions in recorded history when earth tremors have caused the banks of the Jordan to collapse, cutting off the flow of water downstream. But the

> Biblical texts imply that an event does not have to interrupt the laws of nature in order for us to consider it miraculous. *Miracle* can describe any extraordinary happening that people of faith believe to be the result of divine intervention.

biblical text is not interested in the mechanics of the occasion. There is no comment on what was used to dam up the current. The text simply makes a faith claim. Joshua tells the people to remember that "the LORD your God dried up the waters" (4:23). The eyes of faith see the hand of God at work in this event. In the Old Testament, miracles are understood primarily as signs. Their foremost purpose is to point to the nature and the presence of God in human affairs. Both the crossing of the sea in Exodus and the

19

crossing of the Jordan are called signs or miracles in various biblical texts (see Psalm 78:11-13; Joshua 24:17). Both occasions are remembered as times when God intervened in human history.

However, Joshua points out one significant difference between the Exodus from Egypt and the entry into Canaan. With only a few exceptions, the people who participated in the Jordan crossing had not directly experienced the deliverance from Egypt. The people who cross over the Jordan are a generation removed from the saving events of the Exodus. But the LORD is said to "dry up the waters" for this generation just as the LORD "dried up the waters" for the previous generation (Joshua 4:23). Both miracles are performed for the same reasons: so that the people of Israel will "know that among you is the living God" (Joshua 3:10); "so that all the peoples of the earth may know that the hand of the LORD is mighty, and so that you may fear the LORD your God forever" (4:24). See Exodus 14:4, 18, 31 for parallel texts. Perhaps we are meant to conclude that while generations come and go, the nature and the purposes of God's saving action remain the same.

A Heap of Water, a Heap of Stones

Thus the heaping up of the water is conceived of as a sign of God's presence with Israel and as a sign of God's actions on Israel's behalf. In a similar way, the heaping up of the twelve stones is intended to function as a sign as well (4:6). In Joshua 4, the recipients of God's grace erect the sign of stones so that the miraculous sign God performed on their behalf would never be forgotten. The word translated "memorial" in 4:7 is based on the Hebrew root meaning "to remember." God intends for Israel to remember the crossing over into the Promised Land for two specific reasons. First, the stones that are set up to commemorate the Jordan River crossing are intended to keep alive "forever" (4:24) that attitude of reverence and obedience known as "the fear of the LORD."

> The story of Israel's entry into the Promised Land urges us to remember and to proclaim what we see to be God's gracious acts on our behalf.

The second reason is meant to have a larger function. According to Joshua 4:23-24, the LORD enables the people of Israel to cross the Jordan, just as he enabled them to cross over the sea on their way out of Egypt, "so that all the peoples of the earth may know" that the LORD is powerful indeed.

In the story of Rahab, the point was made that those outside of the community of faith may be brought to believe that the LORD "is indeed God in heaven above and on earth below" when they hear what God has done for Israel (Joshua 2:11). Again, in Joshua 4, the story of Israel's entry into the Promised Land urges us to remember and to proclaim what we see to be God's gracious acts on our behalf.

Telling Future Generations

Signs and memorial objects can play an important part in the transmission of faith from one generation to another and from one community to another. But the story of the Jordan River crossing implies that neither miracles nor memorials can fully accomplish their intended purposes without testimonials from people who are willing to interpret and proclaim their meanings.

In order for the signs of faith to function properly, the experiences they stand for must be proclaimed. "You shall let your children know," says the text in Joshua 4:22, echoing "you shall tell them" in 4:7. The rocks set up as a monument may arouse the curiosity of future generations, but it will be up to those who have experienced God's intervention in their lives to tell others what the stones mean.

> We who receive God's saving grace have to make sure to pass on to others the good news of what God has done, is doing, and will do for us and for them.

The chosen people of God must continue to testify, to proclaim what the LORD has done for them, in order that both future generations and the rest of the world may believe.

It may be that some of the signs or memorials we use in the church have become too commonplace, too frequently seen, or too frequently used in a decorative manner to remind us of what God has done for us. Like Israel, we also need memorials capable of prompting our memories and prodding our tongues. We who receive God's saving grace have to make sure to pass on to others the good news of what God has done, is doing, and will do for us and for them.

Dimension 4:
A Daily Bible Journey Plan

Day 1: Joshua 6:15-27

Day 2: Joshua 7:1-15

Day 3: Joshua 7:16-26

Day 4: Joshua 8:1-23

Day 5: Joshua 8:24-35

Day 6: Joshua 9:1-15

Day 7: Joshua 9:16-27

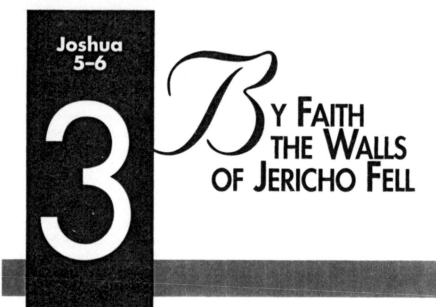

Joshua 5-6

3 BY FAITH THE WALLS OF JERICHO FELL

What to Watch For

Notice the use of phrases such as "to this day" and "ever since" (for instance, in 5:9 and 6:25, as well as in 4:9, 7:26, 8:29, and so on). These phrases are clues that the person who is speaking or writing lives in a later time than the time of the action in the story. The deeds of Joshua may already have been six or seven hundred years in the past before the historians of Israel began to gather their sources together. Because of their efforts we have the story of Israel's entry into Canaan. We do not know exactly what sources were available, but we shall see from the text that the historians were more interested in what God had done to bring Israel into Canaan than in the military activities of their ancestors. The historians have built their reconstruction of the past on a firm foundation of faith. We will find them fully convinced that the conquest of Canaan—from beginning to end—was an act of God, not an accomplishment of the Israelites.

Read Joshua 5 and 6.

1. Who is the unknown person Joshua saw standing on the outskirts of Jericho, and what did he want Joshua to do? (Joshua 5:13-15)

Follow the Lords commands to take the city of Jericho

2. What function did the priests play in the fall of Jericho? (Joshua 6:4-7)

Carried the ark

3. Who ordered the Israelites to devote Jericho and everything in it to destruction? (Joshua 6:15-18)

Joshua

4. What happened to Rahab and her family after the fall of Jericho? (Joshua 6:25)

They lived with the Israelites

Jericho is the oldest known city in the world. It was built around an oasis on the *upper* terrace of the Jordan valley, 825 feet *below* sea level. (Look back at page 17 for a drawing of this unusual geography.) The climate of Jericho and vicinity is warm year-round. Freshwater springs provide water to support date palms, fruit trees, and a variety of other crops. Nearly ten thousand years ago the first settlers built homes in Jericho. They developed an irrigation system capable of supporting a population of over two thousand people. Archaeologists have found the remains of a walled town with a stone tower fortress that dates back to about 8000 B.C. This is the oldest defensive system ever discovered. The site was occupied more or less continuously by various groups of people, from about 8000 to about

23

1600 B.C., when the city was almost completely destroyed. There was no major rebuilding on this location until the seventh century B.C. Some scholars think the oasis was abandoned during this period because the water supply was polluted or infected with a parasite (see 2 Kings 2:19).

Israel's destruction of the city cannot be dated with any degree of certainty. None of the proposed dates for the "conquest" of Canaan (based on either biblical or historical records) fits the archaeological evidence for the destruction of Jericho.

Jericho in Joshua's Time

Whether the deeds of Joshua are dated to the fifteenth or the thirteenth century, archaeology indicates that Jericho was no longer a mighty city in Joshua's time. Long after the site itself was abandoned, however, Jericho remained a powerful symbol of the idolatrous beliefs and practices of Canaan. This suggests that the historians of Israel may have preserved the story of the fall of Jericho for us as an example story.

Biblical example stories speak of real events, but they describe them in figurative rather than in literal terms.

An example story is a cross between a factual report and a parable. It is more concerned with "why" than with "how" or "when." Biblical example stories speak of real events, but they describe them in figurative rather than in literal terms.

The historians, writing from the time of the Exile, may have used the story of the fall of Jericho to shed new light on what was happening or had happened to Israel in the historians' own time. Long before Jerusalem was destroyed by Babylonian invaders, the prophets of Israel warned the people and their leaders that they, too, had "defiled the land" the LORD had given them as an inheritance (see Jeremiah 2:7). As an example story, the destruction of Jericho illustrates the LORD's determination to rid the land of all idolatrous practices (see Deuteronomy 9:4).

Victory Will Be the LORD's

A brief but important scene between Joshua and the "commander of the army of the LORD" in 5:13-15 makes it clear from the beginning of the story that the LORD is in control of the "battle of Jericho." The word translated "army" in 5:14 is in the King James Version (KJV) translated "host." The same word is used in a familiar title for God, the "LORD of hosts." Sometimes the hosts of the LORD are thought to be angelic beings and sometimes they are understood to be the armies of Israel (see 1 Samuel 17:45). In either case, Israel believed that the LORD could lead these hosts into battle against the ungodly.

Before the "battle of Jericho" begins, Joshua sees someone dressed like a soldier prepared for battle (5:13). Joshua challenges the unknown man, asking him, "Whose side are you on?" The stranger refuses to choose sides. In fact, his abrupt answer implies that the question is inappropriate. When the stranger identifies himself as "commander of the army of the LORD," Joshua recognizes his mistake. Joshua knows it is not appropriate to ask whose side God is on. So he quickly changes his question to a more appropriate one: "What does God want me to do?" (see 5:14). As readers, we might expect the messenger of God to say something here about Joshua's role in leading Israel to victory. Instead, the commander of the army of the LORD tells Joshua to remember that the land on which he stands is "holy," echoing the words to Moses at the burning bush (Exodus 3:1-5).

The term translated *holy* in 5:15 means "set apart." Israel was a set-apart people, a people dedicated to the LORD, and the land into which Israel moved was to be set apart for God's purposes as well.

Irrevocably Given to God

The statement in 6:17 that Jericho was "devoted to the LORD for destruction" needs to be understood in relationship to this idea of being set apart.

The New Revised Standard Version (NRSV) uses the phrases "devoted to the LORD for destruction" (as in 6:17, 18, 21) or "utterly destroyed" (as in 2:10, 8:26, and so forth). These expressions are an attempt to translate various forms of the Hebrew word *herem* (HEH-rehm). Other translations refer to "the ban" or to banning things from human usage. *Herem* designates something irrevocably given over to God.

Leviticus 27:28 makes it clear that "every devoted thing is most holy to the LORD." Our dictionaries help us understand the term *devoted* as "entirely given over." You may devote your time, attention, or self to a cause you believe in. To devote (or ban) something to the LORD meant to remove it from ordinary use, to set it aside for God's use (or sometimes for the use of the priests, as in Leviticus 27:28).

Historians living in exile were still confronting the disastrous results of idolatry in their own time. As they placed on scrolls the story of Joshua, they spoke of the ban as a way of cleansing the land of Canaan from the pollution of idolatrous beliefs and practices.

Exodus 22:20 says, "Whoever sacrifices to any god, other than the LORD alone, shall be devoted to destruction." According to Deuteronomy 20:16-18, the purpose of the ban was to remove temptation from Israel. God's people must be prevented from imitating the idolatrous practices of the peoples who were being displaced by Israel's entry into the land (see Deuteronomy 13:6-18). Unfortunately, as

> To devote (or ban) something to the LORD meant to remove it from ordinary use, to set it aside for God's use (or sometimes for the use of the priests, as in Leviticus 27:28).

many other biblical passages make clear, God's people never succeeded in ridding the land of either Canaanite or Israelite forms of idolatry.

The ban (*herem*) was a custom of warfare practiced by other ancient Near Eastern nations as well as by Israel. The Moabite Stone, a monument still in existence, bears an inscription from the mid-ninth century B.C. that refers to a ban practiced by Mesha, king of Moab (who is mentioned in 2 Kings 3). The text is written in Moabite (a language very close to Hebrew). It tells of King Mesha's military exploits. According to Mesha, the Moabite god Chemosh had previously allowed Israel to oppress Moab because Chemosh was angry with Moab. King Mesha says that he placed the Israelite community of Nebo under the ban (using the word *herem*), "devoting them to destruction," to Chemosh, so that Chemosh would allow Mesha to win back land Israel had taken from Moab.

The conversation between Joshua and the commander of the army of the LORD in Joshua 5:13-15 makes it clear that the historians of Israel understood the fall of Jericho to be a part of Israel's "holy war" tradition. The term *holy war* is used by scholars; biblical texts use the phrase "wars of the LORD." (A "Book of the Wars of the LORD" is mentioned in Numbers 21:14.) Either wording describes human conflicts in which the LORD plays a decisive part. In holy war both the battle and the victory are understood to be the LORD's (see 1 Samuel 17:47). Miraculous events (signs and wonders) usually bring victory in holy wars. Human weapons and warriors play a minor part (see Joshua 24:11-12). The Old Testament indicates that the ban was sometimes, but not always, practiced in connection with the "wars of the LORD."

Blow the Ram's Horn, Lift Up the Ark

The ram's horn trumpet (called a *shofar*) was used for both military and religious occasions. It was blown to signal the beginning or the end of a battle or to give news of a victory. But it was also blown to announce or celebrate the presence of the LORD in the midst of the congregation of Israel.

The ark, which played such a prominent part in the story of the crossing of the Jordan, also plays a part in the fall of Jericho. The ark is carried around Jericho in the middle of a liturgical procession. Seven priests, blowing on a special type of trumpet made from a ram's horn, walk in front of the ark and a rear guard walks behind it.

The ram's horn trumpet (called a *shofar*) was used for both military and religious occasions. It was blown to signal the beginning or the end of a battle (Jeremiah 4:19; 2 Samuel 18:16) or to give news of a victory (1 Samuel 13:3). But it was also blown to announce or celebrate the presence of the LORD in the midst of the congregation of Israel (Exodus 19:13, 16, 19;

1 Chronicles 15:28; Psalm 98:6). In Joshua, the blowing of the shofar signals the end, not the beginning of the so-called battle of Jericho. The people shout to celebrate the LORD's victory, not Israel's victory (Joshua 6:16).

Dimension 3:
What Does the Bible Mean to Us?

Many people of faith in both Jewish and Christian communities are often disturbed by reading biblical stories of Israel's entry into the Promised Land. Entire communities are said to have been "utterly destroyed" as Israel moved into Canaan.

What do these texts imply about the nature of God or about God's intervention in human affairs? Do texts such as these give people who consider themselves "holy" permission to engage in the wholesale slaughter of those they consider sinful?

Jesus and a Militant God

Once in a while Christians have mistakenly assumed that the God of the Old Testament was a different being from the God of the New Testament. A careful reading of the New Testament makes clear, however, that Jesus recognized the one he called Father as the same God who acted on Israel's behalf in Old Testament times. Jesus and all the New Testament writers used the Old Testament as their Scripture. Jesus is described as having observed the festivals, laws, and customs of Judaism. He frequently quoted from Old Testament texts (Luke 4:4-12 makes use of Deuteronomy 8:3, 6:13, 6:16, and Psalm 91:11-12 in reporting Jesus' dialogue with the devil. Matthew 22:36-40 quotes from Deuteronomy 6:5 and Leviticus 19:18, and so forth). Thus both Christians and Jews must try to understand how these passages about the ban fit into their common sacred history.

> Jesus recognized the one he called Father as the same God who acts on Israel's behalf in Old Testament times.

Those who handed these stories down to us believed that God worked both through miracles and through natural or human agency. They believed that God could use the culturally conditioned practices of religion and warfare in Joshua's time to intervene in human history.

Does Devotion Mean Sending to Heaven?

In Israel, as well as in neighboring countries, the practice of devoting the spoils of war to the God who ensures the victory seems to be related to the religious understanding of animal sacrifice. The peoples of the ancient

27

Near East apparently believed that things had to be destroyed, slaughtered, or burned in order to transfer them from the earthly to the divine sphere. Many Canaanite peoples sacrificed animals in order to give them as gifts to their god or gods. Israel sacrificed to the LORD in much the same way. The Hebrew word for *sacrifice* has the root meaning "to slaughter."

After the ritual slaughtering of an animal, both Canaanites and Israelites burned either the choicest parts of the meat or the whole body of the animal on an altar. As the flesh went up in smoke, it seemed that the gift was transferred into the spiritual realm. In a similar way, the *herem* (or ban) was based on the idea that everything devoted to destruction (the enemies and all their valuables) became a sacrificial offering to the god of the winning side (see Joshua 6:24).

> God is able to use limited, imperfect tools or agents to accomplish God's intentions.

This explanation assumes that Israel participated fully in the warfare customs of its own time and place and that God chose to work through Israel's customary ways of waging war. Those who offer this explanation of the presence of the ban in our sacred history believe that the human agents used by God to accomplish God's purposes were, and are today, imperfect in many ways. They participate fully in the customs and the prejudices of the times and the cultures in which they live. Nevertheless, the tradition affirms, God is able to use such limited, imperfect tools or agents to accomplish God's intentions.

Descriptions and Prescriptions

Other interpreters suggest that our ancestors in the faith (either in Joshua's time or in the historians' time) misunderstood God's intentions with regard to the Canaanites. Those who participated in the "conquest" of Canaan and/or those who described Israel's entry into the land may have been misled by their own human contexts and customs. They sincerely believed that God commanded or approved of the utter destruction of idolatrous communities. They were mistaken.

Modern readers should note that the biblical stories about the ban are descriptive rather than prescriptive. They describe what happened in a particular time and place. They do not prescribe or encourage others—in all times and all places—to go and do likewise. The stories in Joshua describe a time and a cultural setting in which warfare seemed inevitable. They assume the presence of war; they do not advocate or prescribe it. However, they also assume that definite limits ought to be placed on the conduct of war. The historians were convinced that warriors who fought in the name of the LORD should not receive either riches or glory in return for their efforts. While the practice of *herem* seems gruesome to us, the provisions of the ban did prohibit fighting for personal gain. Devoting the spoils of war to the LORD ensured that no slaughtering and looting would be done for anyone's own glory or private benefit. In Joshua 7:10-26 we will find the story of Achan who "broke faith in regard to the devoted things." The incident illustrates Israel's belief that those who hoped to profit from God's actions against idolatry would bring destruction upon themselves (see 6:18).

The historians of Israel pictured the battle of Jericho as a religious rather than a political event. It was a religious procession, not a siege or a military engagement. Jericho, this timeless symbol of idolatry, was brought to its knees, not by Israel's might, but by the LORD. As the author of Hebrews 11:30 says, "By faith the walls of Jericho fell." But, as Joshua 5:13-15 points out, those who are about to engage in conflicts of faith need to ask the right questions. The real question is not whether God is on our side but whether we are on God's side.

Dimension 4:
A Daily Bible Journey Plan

Day 1: Joshua 10:1-14

Day 2: Joshua 10:15-26

Day 3: Joshua 10:27-43

Day 4: Joshua 11:1-20

Day 5: Joshua 11:21–12:24

Day 6: Joshua 13:1-23

Day 7: Joshua 13:24-33

$\mathcal{F}$ROM HOMELESSNESS TO INHERITANCE

What to Watch For

In this lesson you will examine some of Israel's early attempts to take possession of the land of Canaan. All we can do in one chapter is to sample a few of many texts. If you read carefully you will see that the sources used by the historians apparently did not all agree. When or how soon did the various parts of Canaan come under Israelite control? Statements made in Joshua 11:23 and 21:43, for example, will seem to be in tension with those made in 15:63, 16:10, 17:12-13, and 19:40-47. Some of the passages in this part of Joshua will make it sound as though the whole land was conquered in Joshua's lifetime. Others will give evidence that much of the land remained unconquered long after it was "assigned by lot" to the various tribes of Israel. There will be hints at an underlying theme: the yearning of the homeless for a place to call their own.

This lesson moves quickly through several chapters in the Book of Joshua, stopping briefly to consider the significance of several short passages.

Read all fourteen chapters if you have time and interest, but be sure to read these passages:

Joshua 10:12-14   Joshua 16:10
Joshua 11:21-23   Joshua 17:3-13
Joshua 13:1-7, 13   Joshua 21:43-45
Joshua 15:13-19, 63   Joshua 23:1-5, 14-16

30

1. What ancient book, lost to the present day, included the story of the sun standing still? (Joshua 10:13)

Jasher

2. What is said in Joshua 21:43-45 that seems to be contradicted by what is said or implied by 15:63, 16:10, and 17:12-13?

They couldn't dislodge all the peoples from the land

3. What three words in the statements made in 15:63 and 16:10 tell you about the time in which the speaker (writer) lives?

To this day

4. What do the daughters of Zelophehad and Achsah, daughter of Caleb, have in common? What did each ask for and receive? (Joshua 15:16-19; 17:3-6)

No males, received inheritance of land

Dimension 2:
What Does the Bible Mean?

Land is a central topic in the retelling of Israel's history. The promise of land lured Sarah and Abraham and their descendants into Canaan (see Genesis 12:1-3, 7; 22:17; 28:13). The promise of a land of their own lured Hebrew slaves from Egypt to the wilderness, on the way to Canaan (Exodus 3:17). The Book of Joshua tells us how a homeless people move from landlessness to landedness, from wandering with no permanent home to possessing land that their offspring can inherit.

31

Invasion or Infiltration?

To a disinterested observer, the movement of Israelites into Canaan probably would have looked like many other migrations in the history of humankind. Movements of people from one part of the world to another are often marked both by periods of violent invasion and by quiet infiltration. Newcomers who lay claim to land already occupied may attempt to kill off the earlier inhabitants. Others may enter the area as homesteaders or squatters, laying claim to previously unused or underused land (see Joshua 17:15).

But the people of Israel understand their movement from homelessness to inheritance to be God's doing. Many of the war stories found in Joshua 6–11 emphasize the important role God played in the defeat of various Canaanite forces. God is said to have provided the strategies, the encouragement, and even the miraculous means by which Israel achieved its victories. The brief report in Joshua 10:12-14 quotes a bit of poetry from "the Book of Jashar" (perhaps a fragment of a victory song). That book (pronounced JAY-shuhr) is mentioned here and in 2 Samuel 1:18; but it is otherwise unknown to us, except as one of the sources available to the historians of Israel.

The LORD Indeed Helps Israel

Some interpreters have concluded that an ancient memory of a total eclipse of the sun provided the basis for the statement that the sun stood still. There is no doubt, however, that the author of Joshua 10:12-14 thought the LORD had interfered with the laws of nature at this point in order to bring about Israel's victory over the Amorites.

The established city-states in Canaan had standing armies, trained warriors, and the most sophisticated and effective weapons known in that time and place. In comparison, Israel's forces must have seemed small and poorly equipped. Israel believed its unexpected victories happened against all odds because "the LORD fought for Israel" (10:14; also see 10:42).

It would be a mistake, however, to conclude that Israel's conquest of Canaan was a swift, uncomplicated process. If we skim quickly over the Book of Joshua we may get the impression that Israel swept into Canaan under the leadership of the LORD and conquered the entire geographical area with few (if any) failures. But a more careful reading of the biblical texts shows us that Israel's memories of how the settlement actually happened are more complicated than that.

Allotments to the Twelve Tribes

Chapters 13–21 speak of the "allotment" of territories to the tribes in Israel. Various portions of land were assigned by lot as an inheritance for each family grouping. A random selection process known as the casting or drawing of lots is frequently mentioned in the Bible as a method for answering questions, deciding issues, or determining God's will. Since the land was understood to be the LORD's own possession, given in trust to Israel, the division of the land had to be a religious activity. Thus the story says that "Joshua cast lots for them in Shiloh before the LORD" (18:10) to determine which territories would belong to which tribes. There was to be no squabbling over boundaries because these had been decreed by lot, and the lot was under the LORD's control (Proverbs 16:33).

CASTING LOTS

The Israelites often used lots as a method of determining the will of God. The priest carried two inscribed stones, called Urim and Thummim (lights and perfections), that were thrown in doubtful cases so the entire nation would know God's will. Casting lots was commonly preceded by prayer. The rabbis state that in determining the allotment of the land of Canaan among the tribes two urns were used: "in one were placed tickets with the names of the tribes, and in the other were tickets with the names of the districts. A tribe was drawn and the district that it should possess" (*The New Westminster Dictionary of the Bible;* The Westminster Press, 1970; page 141).

We usually associate the number twelve with the tribes of Israel. Jacob (whose name was later changed to Israel) had twelve sons. Each of these sons is said to be the ancestor of one of the later tribes of Israel. However, the people who traced their ancestry to Joseph were subdivided into two large tribes named after Joseph's sons Manasseh and Ephraim. The descendants of Manasseh were divided again into half-tribes (mentioned in Joshua 13:7-8), one of which was called Machir after Manasseh's first-born son (13:31). The daughters of Zelophehad, who successfully argued for their legal right to inherit their father's portion (Joshua 17:3-4), were the great-great-granddaughters of Machir. Manasseh was also split geographically. One half-tribe of Manasseh (Machir) was assigned territories to the east of the Jordan, along with the tribes of Reuben and Gad (Joshua 13:8). The other portions allotted to Manasseh were to the west of the Jordan. In spite of these tribal subdivisions, the number twelve is kept constant in the allotment of the land because the tribe of Levi was not assigned a territory of its own (Joshua 13:14, 33). The male descendants of Jacob's son Levi were supposed to function as priests with special religious and educational responsibilities within all the tribal boundaries. Thus

Joshua 21 tells us that certain cities and farmlands inside each of the tribal territories were set apart for the use of the Levitical priests and their families.

According to the stories told here, the assignment of tribal borders was mostly done before the land in question was actually conquered by the people of Israel. It was up to the various tribes to take possession of the land allotted to them, by driving out the Canaanites who already lived there. However, the tribes were not always successful in their attempts to drive the Canaanite peoples out of Canaan.

Other Peoples Shared Parts of the Land

A number of passages in both Joshua and Judges report on specific failures. Joshua 15:63 and Judges 1:21 agree that the native Jebusites retained possession of Jerusalem. In fact, Jerusalem remained in Jebusite hands until the time of King David (2 Samuel 5:6-9), a century or more after Joshua died. The Israelites did not drive out the Geshurites or the Maacathites (Joshua 13:13) and the tribe of Ephraim did not drive out the Canaanites who lived in Gezer (Joshua 16:10 and Judges 1:29). Among the Canaanites who continued to live in the territory allotted to Manasseh were the inhabitants of such important ancient cities as Meggido, Dor, and Beth-shean (Joshua 17:11 and Judges 1:27-28).

HOW *DO* YOU SAY THOSE NAMES?

Achsah — AK-suh	**Levi** — LEE-vigh
Beth-shean — beth-SHEE-uhn	**Maacathites** — may-AK-uh-thitez
Dor — dor	**Machir** — MAY-kihr
Ephraim — EE-fray-im	**Manasseh** — muh-NAS-uh
Gad — gad	**Megiddo** — mi-GID-oh
Geshurites — GESH-uh-ritez	**Othniel** — OTH-nee-uhl
Gezer — GEE-zuhr	**Reuben** — ROO-bin
Jebusite — JEB-yoo-site	**Zelophehad** — zuh-LOH-fuh-had

The people of Israel continued to live in the midst of a wide variety of other (often hostile) peoples for many generations after they first began to settle in Canaan. Archaeological records tend to support the view that the settlement of Israel in Canaan was a long, drawn-out process. Sweeping statements such as those found in 11:21-23 and 21:43-45 picture the hoped-for (rather than the actual) fulfillment of God's promises in Joshua's time. Some of the more glowing reports about Israel's complete conquest of the land may come from a later time looking back on the final results of the process. The tribal boundary lines described in Joshua 12–19 actually reflect the political realities of David's time.

Echoes in the Canon

Exodus 33:14 | Joshua 1:13 | Joshua 21:44 | Joshua 22:4 | Joshua 23:1 | Hebrews 4:8-11

Most of the Book of Joshua seems to be concerned with holy wars. Men fought these battles for the possession of land. That land would be passed from generation to generation, from father to son to grandson and so forth. The male line was the genealogical route the historians traced. The historians of Israel seldom mention women's lives or women's actions. However, we find a few brief incidents that shed some light on women's reality in the period of the settlement.

Women and Property Rights

Both the story of Zelophehad's daughters (Joshua 17:3-4) and the story of Achsah (Joshua 15:13-19) occur in more than one location in the biblical text. In Numbers 27:1-11, the five daughters of Zelophehad successfully argue for their legal right to inherit their father's property. In Joshua 17, they remind Joshua that their persistence had brought about a change in the usual laws of inheritance in Israel. However, the tradition also says that they had to promise to marry within their father's kinship group. Then the land they inherited would stay within the same tribal borders (Numbers 36:1-10).

The story of Achsah occurs both in Joshua 15:13-19 and in Judges 1:11-15. Achsah clearly had little or no freedom to choose her own husband. Her father gave her as a victory prize to Othniel, whose allotted land is in the arid wilderness of the Negeb. However, it seems that Achsah gets to own or control the water rights that make her husband's land livable and productive.

Like the story of Rahab, the stories of Achsah and the daughters of

35

Zelophehad indicate that women in this period had some power to act on their own or on their relatives' behalf. Each of the stories shows women taking the initiative to go against the "usual" order of things. As a result they bring about at least a hope of a better future for themselves and their descendants.

Passages from the middle section of Joshua (Chapters 6–23) are seldom studied or read aloud in the church. What Christians know about Israel's "conquest" of Canaan often comes more from hearsay than from a first-hand look at the biblical texts.

The Land of Israel Today

In the modern world who has the right to possess the land that has been called (at various times) Canaan, Israel, or Palestine? The land is cherished as both living space and sacred space by peoples with widely diverse backgrounds and beliefs. Three of the world's monotheistic religions consider this land holy. Judaism and Christianity originated here. Muslims also trace their ancestry to Abraham, through Ishmael, and consider Jerusalem a sacred shrine. The historical tradition that begins with Deuteronomy and ends in Second Kings claims that the land belongs to the LORD (Leviticus 25:23). At first it seemed that God had promised to give the land to Abraham's offspring as "a perpetual holding" (Genesis 12:7; 17:8; and so forth). But as the tradition evolved, the people of Israel began to see that their ability to remain in the land that was given to them would depend on their actions after they gained control over it. The prophets and the historians of Israel were convinced that the Israelites had neither earned nor merited the land they had received from the hand of God (see Deuteronomy 7:7-9; 8:17-20; 9:4-7). The land was given in trust to the people of God only for as long as they were loyal to the LORD and obedient to the law of the LORD (see Deuteronomy 30:15-20). Those to whom the land was entrusted had an obligation to honor its real owner in the ways they conducted their public and private lives on that land (Joshua 23:14-16).

Both the classical prophets and the historians traced Israel's eventual loss of control over the land to disloyalty and disobedience to God. Across the centuries, however, possession of the land passed from one foreign power to another. (Babylonians, Persians, Greeks, Romans, Arabs, and Turkish powers each had their day.) Many Jews continued to believe that "their" land would eventually be restored to them if they remained faithful to the covenant (Deuteronomy 30:1-10).

There was a division of opinion, however. Should Jews wait in trust for God to act on their behalf? Or should they take the initiative to

Across the centuries possession of the Promised Land passed from one foreign power to another. Many Jews continued to believe that "their" land would eventually be restored to them if they remained faithful to the covenant.

secure a homeland for themselves? Those who advocated the creation and maintenance of a Jewish state in Palestine came to be known as Zionists. They began to gain ground around the turn of the twentieth century, leading to the proclamation of the modern state of Israel in 1948.

Christians and a Spiritual Promised Land

Christians consider themselves "heirs according to the promise" made to Abraham (Galatians 3:27-29). Both Christians and Jews believe that God promises an end to the homelessness that plagues humankind. But in Christian circles this promise is usually spiritualized. The biblical references to a promised land take on a symbolic rather than a literal meaning. Some New Testament authors conclude that the promised land in which the people of God will find rest is a "better country, that is, a heavenly one" (Hebrews 11:8-16). However, the Christian tradition continued to insist that this inheritance could only be received as an unmerited gift, not as reward for good behavior. Thus Paul argues that the inheritance promised to Abraham's descendants does not depend on obedience to the law (Romans 4:13-18). We need to be on guard, however, lest we assume that God is only interested in our spiritual inheritance. It is clear that Jesus expects his followers to addresss homelessness in the physical as well as in the spiritual sense. The inheritance that the gospel promises to the children of God is a homeland in which both the body and the spirit can have rest.

> Some New Testament authors conclude that the promised land in which the people of God will find rest is a "better country, that is, a heavenly one."

Dimension 4:
A Daily Bible Journey Plan

Day 1: Joshua 14:1-15

Day 2: Joshua 15:1-19

Day 3: Joshua 15:20-63

Day 4: Joshua 16:1–17:6

Day 5: Joshua 17:7–18:7

Day 6: Joshua 18:8-28

Day 7: Joshua 19:1-31

5

Joshua 9:3-21; 24:1-28

*T*HIS STONE SHALL BE A WITNESS

What to Watch For

In this chapter you will explore what it means to make a covenant. Covenants can be made between two persons or two groups of persons. Covenants can also be between God and human beings. A covenant Israel made with Gibeon, you will see, is considered binding, even though it was based on false pretenses. As for the covenant with God, you will find Joshua calling the tribes of Israel together at Shechem. That was the place where God first promised that the land of Canaan would be home to Abraham's offspring (Genesis 12:6-7). Joshua will summarize the various ways God has intervened in Israel's history (24:2-13). Joshua will challenge the people to pledge themselves exclusively to the LORD. You will find that the primary thing the LORD wants from Israel is loyalty and love in return for what they have already received. You will see traces of doubt in Joshua's mind concerning the people's ability to fulfill their promises. He will caution them against taking this commitment too lightly.

Read two selections from Joshua: 9:3-21 and 24:1-28.

1. What do the Gibeonites want the Israelites to think about them?
(Joshua 9:3-13) What does Deuteronomy 20:10-16 tell us that might
explain why the Gibeonites wanted to deceive Israel?

*That they live far away,
so they wouldn't be killed*

2. List the incidents mentioned in Joshua 24:2-13 that are already familiar
to you from other Bible readings. List incidents previously unknown to
you.

*Familiar Abraham - Isaac Jacob → Eygpt, Eygpt afflicted
- Esau
Red Sea, 40yrs wilderness*

Unknown : Balaam-curse

3. What does Joshua say the people must do if they wish to serve the
LORD? (Joshua 24:14, 23)

Put aside other Gods + be faithful to the Lord

4. What is the purpose of the stone Joshua set up under the oak in the
sanctuary at Shechem? (Joshua 24:26-27)

A reminder of the covenant

The term *covenant* is often used in biblical texts to describe the relationship between God and Israel. When early Christian Bibles were translated
into Latin, the Hebrew word for covenant became the Latin word *testa-
mentum*. Thus the terms "Old Testament" and "New Testament" refer to
the belief that the two sections of the Christian Bible describe an old
covenant and a new covenant between God and the people of God.

The Hebrew word *berit* (ber-EET) is translated "treaty" in Joshua 9
(verses 6, 7, 11, 15, 16) and "covenant" in Joshua 24:25. *Berit* refers to a

COVENANT—
A binding agreement between two or more persons or groups. In the divine covenant God remained on a higher level and made the covenant an act of grace.

binding agreement made between two or more parties (persons or groups). At least one of the parties involved in a covenant promises to act — or not to act — in a specified way. The Old Testament uses the same word to refer both to human agreements (as in Genesis 31:44 or Joshua 9) and to agreements between God and humankind. The term *berit* is used to describe the promises God made to Noah (Genesis 9:11), to Abraham (Genesis 15:18), and to David (2 Samuel 23:5). But most frequently in Jewish and Christian tradition, *berit* refers to the Sinai covenant, the binding agreement made between the LORD and Israel in the wilderness, after the Exodus from Egypt.

Formalized agreements (or covenants) played an important part in the social and political life of the ancient Near East. Archaeologists have uncovered from all over the ancient world a large number of such agreements made between individuals or groups. Covenants were used in the ancient world for marriage agreements, adoptions, and business arrangements. But most of the ancient texts known to us today fall under the category of treaty-covenants. These were binding agreements that spelled out relationships between nations or tribes.

False Information Will Not Cancel a Covenant

Joshua 9 tells us how an enterprising group of Gibeonites tricked the Israelites into making a treaty-covenant. The story implies that such a covenant, once made, was irrevocable. Even though the treaty was made under false pretenses, the Israelites felt bound to keep the promises they had made (9:18-19).

The people of Gibeon lived in the heart of the area that Israel planned to conquer. Israel felt called upon to destroy or to drive out all the native inhabitants who stood between them and the full possession of the land. The people of Gibeon pretended to be travelers from a faraway place who posed no threat to Israel's plan to inherit their land. The leaders of Israel made peace with the Gibeonites, "guaranteeing their lives by a treaty" (9:15). Apparently, Israel was also obligated to defend its new treaty partners from attacks by outsiders. When the Gibeonites were later threatened by a coalition of Amorite kings, the Israelites came to their aid (Joshua 10:6).

Thus it seems that the people of Israel and the peoples of Canaan had a similar understanding of the nature and the purposes of treaty-covenant agreements. Even the ritual actions that accompanied the making of the covenant between Israel and Gibeon resemble those practiced by neighboring nations. The sharing of food (Joshua 9:14) and the swearing of oaths before God (9:15) played a part in most ancient Near Eastern covenant-making ceremonies.

Joshua 24 tells the story of a somewhat different type of covenant agreement made at Shechem, an ancient site in the central highlands between Mount Gerizim and Mount Ebal. As was the case on Mount Sinai (see Exodus 24), one of the parties involved in the Shechem covenant-making ceremony was "the LORD, the God of Israel." ("All the tribes of Israel" were invited.) In outward form, the making of this covenant follows the common, customary conventions of covenant-making in the secular culture. Scholars have often noted that both the Sinai covenant and the covenant described in Joshua 24 bear a remarkable resemblance to international treaties made between Near Eastern nations in the period from 1500 to 1100 B.C.

When Israel wanted to describe the ways they felt committed to the LORD, they used language borrowed from the common political and legal agreements of the culture in which they lived. They adopted vocabulary and forms familiar to them from social and political settings and used them for religious purposes.

Most of the ancient Near Eastern treaties available for comparison with biblical covenants are suzerainty treaties. A "suzerain" (SOO-zer-an) is a great and powerful ruler who allows less powerful parties to enter into a privileged relationship with him. The suzerain promises to support and protect his less powerful allies (who are called vassals). In return, the suzerain expects the vassal to give loyalty and service to him and to all his concerns.

Such treaties ordinarily begin with the self-identification of the suzerain, who then lists all the things that the suzerain has done in the past for the benefit of the vassal. The historical recital assumes that gratitude should make the recipient of such favors feel obligated to do what the benefactor wants done. It also implies that there are conditions attached to the continuance of this relationship between the superior and the inferior parties. If the vassal wishes to continue receiving protection from the suzerain, the vassal must agree to do certain things in return. The stipulations vary from treaty to treaty, but the vassal is almost always asked to pledge exclusive loyalty to the suzerain who offers the vassal this chance to continue their past and present relationship.

In Return for Everything, Do One Thing!
In Joshua 24:2-13, the LORD is identified as the God of Israel (verse 2). Joshua then proceeds to list all the LORD's actions on Israel's behalf (verses 3-13). Israel is asked to do only one thing in return for everything God has done. The LORD demands exclusive loyalty from Israel (verse 14).

SIMILARITIES BETWEEN ANCIENT NEAR EASTERN AND BIBLICAL COVENANTS

Typical Elements in Ancient Near Eastern Covenants	Similar Elements in Joshua 2
Covenant-Giver Is Identified: "These are the words of Mursilis, the Great King, King of Hatti . . ."	Joshua 24:2: "Thus says the LORD the God of Israel"
Historical Prologue	Joshua 24:2-13
Stipulations of Loyalty	Joshua 24:14, 19-20, 23-24
Other Conditions/Stipulations	Joshua 24:25
Provisions for Making Permanent Record	Joshua 24:26
Record to Be Kept in a Holy Place (in the temple of the god worshiped by the covenant partners)	Joshua 24:26
List of Witnesses to the Treaty (often includes inanimate objects)	Joshua 24:22, 27
Statement of Rewards and Punishments for Obedience or Disobedience to Agreed-upon Conditions (often expressed as blessings and curses)	Joshua 24:19-20

Israel is asked to do only one thing in return for everything God has done: give the LORD exclusive loyalty.

Joshua is aware of how difficult it will be for the people of Israel to devote themselves exclusively to the service of the LORD. Their ancestors had made similar pledges and had failed to keep them. And even the people who were gathered here at Shechem, the people who willingly acknowledged their indebtedness to the LORD (24:16-18), must have had some divided loyalties. Joshua tells them twice to put away the foreign gods that were still among them (24:14, 23).

Joshua clearly warns the people that pledging themselves to an exclusive relationship with the LORD is a risky business. Their oath of loyalty, once given, cannot be withdrawn. Noncompliance with the terms of this binding agreement will be severely punished (verse 20).

The covenant made at Shechem apparently included some other stipulations as well, but the content of these "statutes and ordinances" is not spelled out for us. The details of the covenant were preserved in writing "in the book of the law of God" (24:26), and a stone was set up to memorialize the agreement. The stone was set up "under the oak in the sanctuary of the LORD" at Shechem, in the very place where God had first told Abraham that this land would belong to his numerous offspring (Genesis 12:7). The promise of land has come full circle. The covenant made at Shechem acknowledges Israel's indebtedness to the giver of the gift of land.

Dimension 3: What Does the Bible Mean to Us?

How can we speak to one another about God's love for us? How can we describe the transforming power of God's spirit in our lives? We have to use human words and draw analogies from human experience. The people of Israel knew they were both chosen by God and bound to God in a special relationship. To describe the way they felt they used analogies drawn from ordinary, familiar human experiences.

Other Biblical Analogies

The treaty-covenant analogy is one of many analogies the Bible uses to describe God-human relationships. Elsewhere the bond between God and Israel is compared to that between parent and child or between marriage partners. These analogies all have one essential ingredient in common. Each says God is bound to humankind by love, not by obligation. God and Israel are bound together by God's love. Each case indicates that the appropriate human response would be to return that love to God.

> God is bound to humankind by love, not by obligation. God and Israel are bound together by God's love.

A covenant is understood in Christian tradition as a tie that both binds and frees those who enter into it. The Greek translation of the Hebrew Scriptures uses the Greek word *diatheke* (dee-ath-AY-kay) to translate the Hebrew word *berit*. In the Greek-dominated culture *diatheke* was used to refer to freeing slaves from human bondage by "willing" them to the service of a god or a temple. For the slave, being bound over to a god meant being freed from forced servitude to another human being.

The New Testament authors may have understood the term *diatheke* in the phrase *new covenant*. The way to be free from bondage to sin is to be bound in covenant with the LORD.

> The way to be free from bondage to sin is to be bound in covenant with the LORD.

It seems evident from Joshua 9 that Israel was familiar with the treaty conventions that functioned in its own historical time and place. Treaty-making was a common experience among Middle Eastern peoples. Joshua 24 draws an analogy between this familiar human activity and the type of commitment Israel felt existed between itself and the LORD.

Covenant relationships are much less familiar to us in the modern world. The institution of marriage retains some covenantal aspects, but a commitment to the concept of marriage as a binding, permanent relationship is becoming increasingly rare. The process of adopting a child may come closer in our experience to what Israel meant by the covenant bond between God and the people of God. Some ancient treaties actually use the terms *father* and *son* to designate the parties to the covenant. Like an adoption process, a covenant resembles a legal contract in some ways. Both covenants and legal contracts contain binding agreements, but partners in a contract are bound only by what can be spelled out in the stipulations. A covenant asks the parties involved to enter into a relationship that goes far beyond legal obligations.

The Covenant Way: Love and Loyalty

First and foremost a covenant calls for love and loyalty between the parties entering into the relationship. Loyalty to one's covenant partner cannot be limited to or defined solely as obedience to specific rules and regulations.

In many ways, the treaty-covenant form is a particularly appropriate one for Israel to use in talking about its relationship with God. In many suzerainty treaties the vassal was called upon to "love" and be faithful in service to the overlord. This formal element is echoed in Israel's covenant traditions when Moses says, "Love the LORD your God with all your heart, and with all your soul, and with all your might" (Deuteronomy 6:5), and when Joshua says, "Incline your hearts to the LORD, the God of Israel" (24:23). In Israel's traditions the people's obligations to love God is primary. The rest of the covenant stipulations (which are mentioned but not spelled out in Joshua 24) may have told the people of God how the love of God should apply to their day-to-day lives. Joshua 24:26 says that Joshua wrote these "words" (*devarim*) in the book of the law of God. The same Hebrew term is used to describe the "ten words" (Ten Commandments), which were kept in the ark of the covenant. Thus it is possible that the words Joshua recorded were similar in content to Exodus 20:1-17 and Deuteronomy 5:6-21.

Both the Sinai covenant and the Shechem covenant emphasize the exclusiveness of the love Israel is asked to return to God. If Israel wants to receive the freedom that comes from being bound to God in covenant, Israel must agree not to worship, to bow down to, or to "serve" other gods (see Exodus 20:3-6; Deuteronomy 5:7-10; Joshua 24:14, 20, 23). Idolatry is the ultimate covenant violation.

Prohibitions against idolatry may seem to have little relevance for Christians today. Very few Christians think they have idols in their homes.

Very few think they have bowed down to other gods. But if the essence of idolatry is disloyalty to God, as the covenant traditions suggest, then idolatry is in fact still rampant in many Christian lives.

> If the essence of idolatry is disloyalty to God, as the covenant traditions suggest, then idolatry is in fact still rampant in many Christian lives.

The treaty-covenant tradition is concerned with maintaining the well-being of the kingdom that is under the covenant-giver's protection. Disloyalty in that context includes anything that shows a disregard for God's agenda in the world. If our Sovereign is concerned for the well-being of all creation, then anything we do that harms the created world is an act of disloyalty on our part.

The question of ultimate loyalty might also be phrased in terms of what (or whom) we trust to guarantee our own well-being. To put more trust in medicine, in modern science, in government, or in wealth than in God is the essence of idolatry.

Dimension 4:
A Daily Bible Journey Plan

Day 1: Joshua 19:32-51

Day 2: Joshua 20:1–21:19

Day 3: Joshua 21:20-45

Day 4: Joshua 22:1-20

Day 5: Joshua 22:21-34

Day 6: Joshua 23:1-16

Day 7: Joshua 24:1-13

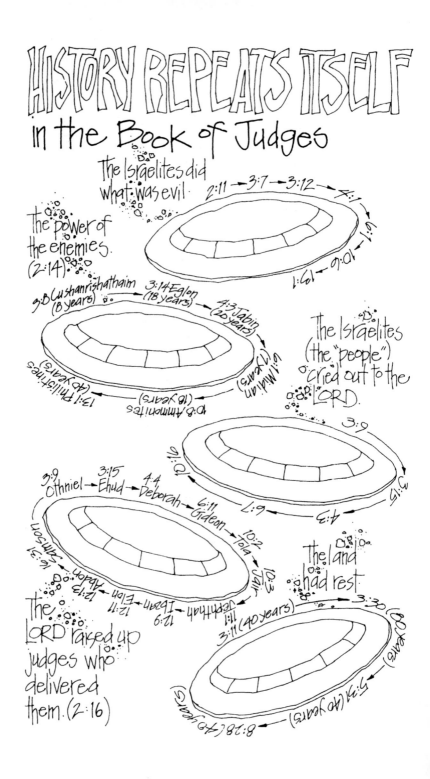

HISTORY REPEATS ITSELF

in the Book of Judges

The Israelites did what was evil. 2:11 → 3:7 → 3:12 → 4:1

The power of the enemies. (2:14)

The Israelites (the "people") cried out to the LORD. 3:9

The LORD raised up judges who delivered them. (2:16)

The land had rest.

3:8 Cushanrishathaim (8 years) — 3:14 Eglon (18 years) → 4:3 Jabin (20 years)

3:9 Othniel → 3:15 Ehud → 4:4 Deborah → 6:11 Gideon → 10:2 Tola → 10:3 Jair → 11:1 Jephthah → 12:9 Ibzan → 12:11 Elon → 12:13 Abdon → 13:31 Samson

3:11 (40 years) — 3:30 (80 years) — 4:24 — 5:31 (40 years) — 8:28 (40 years)

HISTORY REPEATS ITSELF

What to Watch For

As we move into the Book of Judges we will read about the areas Israel conquered or failed to conquer after Joshua died. We will find that Israel's failure to bring the whole land under their control was explained as the result of their failure to keep their covenant with the LORD. In Judges 2:11-21 you will find the period summarized. You will realize that the historians who collected the records and memories saw in those early years in Canaan a circular pattern in Israel's behavior and in the LORD's response.

You will notice that "judges" in this period did not hear and decide cases of law. Instead, the judges were asked to "deliver" Israel from oppression (see 2:16, 18; 3:9, 15). We will discover that little is known about the first judge, Othniel, and we may learn more than we want to about the second judge, Ehud; but unpleasant tales are part of biblical history.

Read the first three chapters of Judges for the whole story.

Dimension 1:
What Does the Bible Say?

1. What specific things did the people do to anger the LORD? (Judges 2:11-13)

Followed + worship other Gods
Baal + Ashtoreths

2. What did the LORD do to punish the people? (Judges 2:14-16, 21-23)

Let raiders from other tribes "plunder them"

3. When the LORD "raised up judges" what relationship did the LORD maintain with them? (Judges 2:18)

He was with them + allowed them to live

4. How would you describe the story of Ehud to someone who had never heard it? What kind of a story is it? (Judges 3:12-30)

Not as graphic detail

Dimension 2:
What Does the Bible Mean?

In the Book of Joshua the incompleteness of the conquest was thought of as a temporary state that the LORD would overcome in due time. But after the death of Joshua and his generation, the warning given in Joshua 23:16 turned into the reality described in Judges 2:11-15, 19-20. According to 2:22-23, the LORD had left some of the pagan nations in place in Joshua's time "in order to test Israel." Israel flunked the test. God's promise of a place of rest in Canaan collided with the people's failure to keep their covenant promises.

The Canaanite fertility religions seem to have included sexual inter-course with sacred prostitutes (both male and female) as a part of the cultic rites. Thus following the gods of Canaan would have involved both idol-worship and immorality according to the covenant codes.

In Judges, Chapters 2–16, the historian describes this period in the history of Israel in a series of vicious circles. The pattern is outlined in 2:11-21: The people sin, the LORD punishes them by allowing their enemies to oppress them, the people cry out to the LORD in their distress, and the LORD responds by raising up a judge who frees them from oppression. But whenever the judge dies, the people fall back into their sinful ways and the cycle begins all over again. There are few

WHO'S WHO AMONG THE IDOLS?

Israel's hope to conquer the whole of the Promised Land was shattered. The new generations of Israel abandoned the LORD and worshiped the "Baals" (BAY-uhls), the "Astartes" (as-TAHR-tees, 2:13), and the "Asherahs" (uh-SHIHR-uhz, 3:7).

Baal was the name of the principal fertility god in Canaan. He seems to have been worshiped in many localized forms. As the god of the storm he controlled the rains. His sacred animal was the bull, who symbolized power and fertility. Baal is sometimes portrayed riding or standing on his sacred bull.

Astarte was a goddess associated with love, fertility, and war. The Babylonians called her Ishtar, Queen of Heaven; and she was worshiped in Phoenicia and in Egypt as well as in Canaan.

Asherah can refer to a mother-goddess (thought to be the mother of Baal and a number of lesser gods). An Asherah can also be a cult object associated with the mother-goddess. Although these objects are never described, they seem to have been some form of wooden pole, representing either the goddess or her sacred tree. In the story of Gideon, the New Revised Standard Version translates the word *asherah* as "sacred pole" (Judges 6:25-26).

surprises in this presentation of Israel's early history. History repeats itself. Backsliding seems inevitable as long as other peoples and other gods remain in the land.

> History repeats itself. Backsliding seems inevitable as long as other peoples and other gods remain in the land.

Judges to the Rescue

Twelve judges are named in Judges 3–16. The six who have stories attached to their names are Othniel, Ehud, Deborah, Gideon, Jephthah, and Samson. Their stories have been strung together like beads on a chain, interspersed with cycles of sin, oppression, and redemption. Shamgar (3:31), Tola and Jair (10:1-5), and Izban, Elon, and Abdon (12:8-15) remain in the background of Israelite history because we are told so little about them or their historical circumstances. Only Shamgar and Tola are said to have delivered Israel. The others are said only to judge (that is, perform minor governmental functions).

The term translated *to judge* actually means to rule or to govern. In

Israel, as well as in other parts of the ancient Near East, rulers were expected to deal with both law and order. Kings proclaimed and administered the law of the land. Judging between competing claims was simply a part of keeping order in the realm. But the Book of Judges recalls a time when there were no officially designated rulers in Israel (Judges 21:25).

After Joshua died the various tribes scattered to their diverse territories. There were no centralized or organized forms of government. Each of the major judges is said to rise up from the midst of social, political, and religious chaos. Each seems to have derived some governmental authority based on his or her ability to gain a period of rest for the land (3:11, 30).

After Samson's death in Chapter 16, no more judges are mentioned until Samuel is said to judge Israel in 1 Samuel 7. But the stories in Judges 17–21 indicate that political, social, and religious chaos was still the order of the day.

Finding Something to Laugh About

Many of the stories in Judges are told in a humorous manner. Unfortunately, it is not easy for those who read the biblical texts in translation to recognize the puns and the ironic twists of language that lent a note of laughter to the telling in its original tongue. The stories of Othniel and Ehud poke fun at Israel's enemies by giving the defeated kings mocking nicknames. The name "Cushan-rishathaim from Aram-naharaim" (3:8) sounds like a pun in Hebrew meaning "Double Trouble from Twin Rivers." The Moabite king killed by Ehud is called "Eglon," meaning "Little Fat Calf." He is described as being "very fat" (3:17). In Hebrew, the word translated "fat" also has the negative meaning of "complacent." The name assigned to this particular king of Moab may have had some basis in reality. But the Hebrew narrator has probably altered the name of the king slightly in order to make fun of this oppressor of Israel.

The story of Ehud, like that of Othniel, contains an extended play on words using the various senses of the Hebrew word *yad*. Literally, *yad* means "hand"; but it can be used to imply power, control, or agency. Ehud is said to be "a Benjaminite." Although *Benjamin* is a common tribal designation, the word itself means "son of the right hand." But

Ehud is also said to be either a left-handed man or a man who could not use his right hand. The Hebrew term literally means that his right hand was bound. We do not know if Ehud's left-handedness is natural or induced. The right arms of young children may have been bound to encourage left-handedness, to give a soldier some advantage in battle. The phrase "bound in his right hand" might also have described an actual physical impairment. But in any case, Ehud's tribal identity contrasts ironically with his physical makeup.

The word *yad* is used five times in this short story. First the narrator introduces Ehud to us as a left-handed member of the "sons of the right hand." Then we hear that Israel sent tribute to Eglon "by Ehud's hand" (NRSV translates "by him" in verse 15) and that Ehud uses his left hand to kill the Moabite king (verse 21). When Ehud escapes unharmed he tells his people "the LORD has given your enemies into your hand" (verse 28), and the story concludes with the statement that Moab "was subdued that day under the hand of Israel."

By using the word *hand* so frequently the narrator reminds us that the hand of God is at work throughout the story. Both Eglon the Moabite and Ehud the Benjaminite are said to be agents of God. When the Israelites turned away from the LORD, after Othniel died, "the LORD strengthened King Eglon of Moab against Israel" (3:12). But when the people cried out to God, after eighteen years of suffering under King Eglon for their sins, "the LORD raised up for them a deliverer, Ehud son of Gera" (3:15). The Moabite king is raised up as an agent of God's punishment, and he is knocked down by God's new agent of deliverance. The narrator implies that Eglon grew fat and complacent in his advantaged position. He grew to expect tribute from his underlings as a matter of course. He began to take his favored position for granted. The "secret message" Ehud delivers to Eglon is a message appropriate for Israel as well: this is what happens when the agents of God grow complacent.

There is a warning for all people of faith hidden in the historian's reconstruction of events of the period. The people of God are always in danger of resembling Eglon. Whenever the faith community begins to grow complacent there is a risk of ending up like Eglon. A new and unexpected agent of God knocks us from our positions of power.

> Whenever the faith community begins to grow complacent there is a risk of ending up like Eglon—fat and complacent. Then a new and unexpected agent of God knocks us from our positions of power.

The judges were agents of God's grace in an idolatrous world.

The enemies of Israel had earthly kings who could proclaim laws and enforce them. The kings could muster armies and command them. But Israel's king was supposed to be the LORD, to whom they had pledged their allegiance in the treaty-covenants of Sinai and Shechem (Joshua 24).

As a king with loyal subjects, the LORD could easily have driven the nations out before Israel (Judges 2:3). But the people of Israel could not move forward and possess all the Promised Land without the direction that could have been provided by God and the covenant commandments. Thus the historians describe the people spinning in circles of sin and misery with brief interruptions provided by the mercy of God. The judges were agents of God's grace in an idolatrous world.

Right in Their Own Eyes

The historians of Israel, looking back from the time of the monarchy, commented unfavorably on the whole period of the judges: "In those days there was no king in Israel; all the people did what was right in their own eyes" (Judges 21:25). Thus we should not be surprised to find that the majority of stories included in this history of Israel's sin are negative example stories.

Often even the judges who are called upon to deliver God's people from the consequences of their folly are presented as less than admirable.

Each narrative preserved in Judges illustrates the weakness of a people who have abandoned their unifying allegiance to the LORD. In many cases, even the judges who are called upon to deliver God's people from the consequences of their folly are presented as less than admirable.

Ehud, for example, does not act in a particularly heroic way. It is clear that his success in liberating Israel from Moab depends on trickery and deceit. He uses his left-handedness (or his inability to use his right hand) to lull his enemies into trusting him alone with Eglon. He prepares a special weapon (with two sharp edges) and hides it under his clothing, on his right thigh. He tricks Eglon into giving him a private audience; and he catches the king in a vulnerable position. (A "cool roof chamber" [Judges 3:20] seems in verse 24 to be sort of an outhouse.)

Humor in Difficult Days

Our taste in humor has improved across the centuries. We may find it hard to believe that the earliest audiences for this story laughed over the antics of Ehud and enjoyed the humiliation of Eglon. The further removed we are from the original speaker's setting in life, the harder it is for us to determine if something was meant to be funny. But there are several indications in the text that the story of Ehud and Eglon intended to provoke laughter among Israelite audiences.

Modern readers often do not think of humor in connection with the biblical text. Popular piety conditions us to expect only serious, straight-forward communications related to our faith. We seldom expect to be entertained by Scripture, and so we are not. Word-plays and puns abound in the Bible, but it is difficult for us to detect verbal humor in translation from one language to another.

> The Old Testament actually contains a wide variety of humor. But we seldom expect to be entertained by Scripture, so we are not.

The Old Testament actually contains a wide variety of humor. Some things are simply meant to be funny, without any particular purpose except to catch the attention and the memory of the audience. Since almost nothing is recorded about several of the judges, some persons might find a bit of humor by looking at three of them together. Jair had thirty sons and thirty donkeys (10:3-4). Ibzan had thirty sons and thirty daughters (12:8). Abdon had forty sons, thirty grandsons, and seventy donkeys (12:13).

The Use of Tendency Wit

But most of the humor in the biblical text is tendency wit. The term *tendency wit* refers to humor used to make a point, to serve a purpose, as well as to invoke laughter. Tendency wit can be aimed at oneself and one's own group or it can be aimed at another. Whether we find such wit funny usually depends on the kind of attitude we have toward the target of the humor. Does the butt of the joke deserve retribution? Do we think our own or someone else's pretension needs to be "taken down a peg"?

We usually do not approve when members of a dominant group use wit to bolster their own status in relationship to a subordinate group. But we think it is acceptable for members of an oppressed community to make fun of their oppressors (unless we are the oppressors).

Humor can be used by the downtrodden (the underdogs in any setting) to keep alive the spirit of resistance. Victims of oppression can use wit as a weapon to preserve and strengthen their sense of self-respect.

> Even when we know we should love our enemies and do good to those who persecute us, we cannot help smiling when we hear that our oppressors have received their just deserts.

In Judges 3:12-30, we have an example of Israelite tendency wit directed against Israel's long-time enemy. Moab, Ehud, like Israel, is the underdog in this situation. The odds would be against him in an open conflict. So he uses trickery and deceit to even the odds and give Israel a chance to win the battle against a stronger and an oppressive power.

To appreciate Ehud's tactics, a modern reader would have to identify imaginatively with Ehud's situation. To see any humor in the humiliating murder of Eglon, we have to imagine ourselves suffering as much as Israel suffered under Moabite rule. Even when we know we should love our enemies and do good to those who persecute us, we cannot help smiling when we hear that our oppressors have received their just deserts.

Maybe God wanted us to learn that God can send help from unexpected quarters.

We are not told why the LORD chose Ehud to deliver Israel from the Moabites. Nor will we be told what attracted the LORD to any of the other judges. But it seems that many of those whom God used to liberate Israel were unlikely candidates for the job. Perhaps no real heroes were available in such sinful times. Even the judges may have been diminished by the times in which they lived. Or maybe God wanted us to learn from the stories in Judges that God can send help from unexpected quarters, in ways we least expect it. To human eyes the judges usually seem to be unlikely candidates to become the agents of God's grace in a sinful world.

Dimension 4:
A Daily Bible Journey Plan

Day 1: **Joshua 24:14-28**

Day 2: **Joshua 24:29-33; Judges 2:6-15**

Day 3: **Judges 1:1-21**

Day 4: **Judges 1:22-36**

Day 5: **Judges 2:1-5, 16-23**

Day 6: **Judges 3:1-11**

Day 7: **Judges 3:12-30**

TURNING EXPECTATIONS UPSIDE DOWN

What to Watch For

We will learn how Deborah, Barak, and Jael are able to defeat Israel's enemies. Immediately following the prose account, a poem, actually a song of victory, will celebrate the same happening. Continue to look for the pattern of sin and oppression outlined in the previous chapter. Pay careful attention to the description of Deborah, called a prophetess, who was judging Israel. Although Deborah and Barak are the Israelites who will lead the tribes into battle, you will discover that a non-Israelite woman named Jael will accomplish the defeat of Sisera. Once again we shall see that Israel's victories are the work of the LORD. The poetry in 5:8-18 will praise the Israelite tribes who came to help and will mock those who did not fight against the Canaanites.

Be sure to read and compare the prose version (Judges 4) and the poetic version (Judges 5) of the story of Deborah, Barak, and Jael.

Dimension 1: What Does the Bible Say?

1. How does Barak respond to Deborah's call to arms? Why do you think he responds to Deborah in this way? (Judges 4:6-9)

2. Compare the two versions of the battle against Sisera's army in 4:12-16 and 5:19-21. What is said to cause the enemy to flounder?

3. Compare the ways the two chapters describe what Jael does. How do they differ? What elements remain the same in both versions? (4:17-22; 5:24-27)

4. What is the point made by Judges 5:28-30? Why is this picture of Sisera's mother included in the poem?

5. What similarities do you see between the stories of Ehud (3:15-25) and Jael?

Dimension 2:
What Does the Bible Mean?

Deborah is introduced to us in the prose narrative as both a prophetess and a judge (4:4). She seems to have been a judge in the more traditional sense of the word: people came to her to settle disputes. Female prophets are mentioned elsewhere in the biblical tradition (Miriam, Exodus 15:20; Huldah, 2 Kings 22:14-20; Noadiah, Nehemiah 6:14; and Anna, Luke 2:36-38).

The Role of a Prophet
Women who are prophets interpret and communicate the will of God, just as male prophets do. Often their words are remembered because they are put in poetic form. Always the thrust of their message is, "Thus says the LORD." Deborah acts in a typically prophetic way as she tells Barak what the LORD commands him to do (4:6-7).

We are not told why Barak refuses to go to battle without Deborah by his side. It may be that he has too little confidence in the word of God. Or it may be that he has too little confidence in Deborah. He may want her to back up her confident words by going with him into battle. In any case, Deborah's response indicates that Barak's reputation will suffer because of his refusal to go alone. Since he insists on having a woman's help, credit for the victory will go to a woman (4:9).

> Prophets interpret and communicate the will of God. Often their words are remembered because they are put in poetic form. Always the thrust of their message is, "Thus says the LORD."

Female prophets give us our earliest examples of Israel's music. When Miriam is called a prophet in Exodus 15:20-21, she is also shown singing a victory song, similar in many ways to the song Deborah sings. Both Miriam's song and Deborah's song include the phrase "sing to the LORD," indicating that their songs are meant to be religious in orientation (Exodus 15:21; Judges 5:3). Both Miriam's song and Deborah's song reflect back on an event that has already happened. They interpret and comment on the meaning of the event for the people of Israel.

Thus it seems that Judges 4 reports a significant event in Israel's history, and Judges 5 comments on that event. The song in Chapter 5 is sung in response to the event, after the battle is over and the victory has been won.

The Canaanite city of Hazor and Barak's city of Kadesh were both located north of the Sea of Galilee, in the territory Joshua assigned to Naphtali. The battle between Sisera and the Israelites takes place southwest of the Sea of Galilee, in the Kishon valley between Mount Tabor and the fortress-city of Megiddo, in the territory assigned to Zebulun. In Judges 4:6, only the tribes of Naphtali and Zebulun are included in Deborah's call to arms. The narrator knows that Jael, who will emerge as the key figure in this story, belongs to a clan usually located near the southern end of the Dead Sea, much farther south than the Kishon valley (see Judges 1:16). So 4:11 explains how Jael's family of Kenites found themselves camped in the midst of a struggle between peoples living around the Sea of Galilee.

The LORD Causes a Panic

The battle itself is pictured in vague, impressionistic terms. The Hebrew word *nachal* can mean either a flow of water or the ravine in which it runs. The same word is called a "wadi" in 4:7 and 13 and translated as "torrent" in 5:21. The prose text may imply that Sisera and his chariots were lured into a dry riverbed or a narrow ravine, where their chariots of iron became more of a handicap than an advantage in the fighting. According to 4:15,

57

the tide of the battle turned (in typical holy war tradition) when "the LORD threw Sisera and all his chariots and all his army into a panic."

The poetic text implies that a sudden rainstorm followed by a flash flood (5:4 and 5:20-21) trapped the Canaanites between the "torrent" and the Israelites, who held the higher ground (4:14), Sisera is said to escape on foot (4:16), which might imply that his chariot was disabled or bogged down in the mud.

The Song of Deborah pictures Israel not as a unity but as a loosely organized confederation of tribes who may or may not come to one another's aid when help is called for.

The historical notice in 4:1-3 speaks of Israel as a unity: Israel did what was evil, Israel was punished, and Israel cried out. But both the prose story and the song of Deborah indicate that this time of crisis did not involve all Israel. Only two tribes are mentioned in the prose of Chapter 4 (Naphtali and Zebulun). Ten tribes are mentioned by name in the song in Chapter 5. Ephraim, Benjamin, Machir (part of Manasseh), Zebulun, Issachar, and Naphtali are praised for their help. Reuben, Gilead (or Gad), Dan, and Asher are criticized for failure to participate. Judah and Levi are not mentioned at all. The Song of Deborah pictures Israel not as a unity but as a loosely organized confederation of tribes who may or may not come to one another's aid when help is called for.

The narrative in Chapter 4 emphasizes the role God plays in the outcome of the conflict. God promises to lure Sisera into the ravine (4:7) and to give the victory to the Israelites (4:7, 14). The LORD induces the panic that turns the tide of the battle (4:15). The story concludes, "So on that day God subdued King Jabin of Canaan before the Israelites" (4:23).

In contrast, the poetic version of the story emphasizes the roles human beings played in the conflict. The song does note that "the stars fought from heaven . . . against Sisera" (5:20), but far more space is devoted to the earthly powers who either supported or did not support the LORD's cause. The song praises the people (5:2) and the commanders (5:9) who offer themselves willingly in times of crisis. It praises Deborah who "arose as a mother in Israel" to prod her offspring into action just when she was most needed (5:7). And it condemns those who did not "come to the help of the LORD, to the help of the LORD against the mighty" (5:23).

The Israelite town of Meroz did not join in the battle and receives a curse (Judges 5:23). Jael, a non-Israelite woman, went out of her way to "come to the help of the LORD." She receives a blessing (5:24).

The cursing of Meroz in 5:23 is followed immediately with the blessing of Jael in 5:24. The contrast is striking. The Israelite town of Meroz did not join in the battle. But Jael, a non-Israelite woman, went out of her way to "come to the help of the LORD" in this time of chaos and crisis.

58

The prose account pictures Jael's action as a clever trick. An aside in 4:17 tells us that there was peace between King Jabin of Hazor and the Kenite clan to which Jael belonged. When Sisera fled the scene of the battle, where his soldiers were being slaughtered by the Israelites, he expected to find a safe hiding place among Jabin's allies. But even if there had not been peace between them, Jael's offer of hospitality would have been understood as an offer of protection, according to the customs of the time. Jael lulls Sisera into a false sense of security. She tells him not to be afraid (4:18). She gives him milk to drink (4:19), covers him with a rug, and then waits until he is asleep before she kills him, driving the tent peg through his head into the ground (4:21).

The Poem's Graphic Language

But the poem gives us the impression that Jael's attack took both courage and daring. In the poem Sisera is pictured as awake and upright when Jael strikes him down. The scene is described with dramatic repetitions, so that we see it almost in slow motion:

"He sank, he fell,
   he lay still at her feet;
at her feet he sank, he fell;
   where he sank there he fell dead" (5:25).

There is an abrupt change of scene in 5:28. Immediately after Sisera dies, the singer tells us what Sisera's mother is doing as her son lies dead at Jael's feet. With a touch of bitter irony, the singer of the song imagines Sisera's mother looking out a window, wondering why her son has not yet come home. The image of a woman looking out of a latticed window is a common one in ancient Near Eastern art and literature.

The singer in Judges 5 tells us that while Sisera is dying an unheroic death at the hand of a woman, another woman is imagining that he and his troops are still busy looting and raping their victims (5:29-30). The phrase that the New Revised Standard Version (NRSV) translates "a girl or two for every man" (in 5:30) has a more brutal sound in the original Hebrew. The women quoted here are said to take the common warfare practices of their time for granted. The women of Hazor expect the common practice: women on the losing side will be brutally raped and despoiled. According to the singer of this song, Sisera's mother and her companions both condone and plan to benefit from the spoils of war (5:30).

There is an ironic match between what Sisera and his mother expect and what they get. The word used to describe Sisera's end is not the ordinary word for death. The word that NRSV translates

Sisera, the would-be despoiler of women, is despoiled by a woman. And the mother who expects to gain spoils from her son's violence loses both the spoils and the son.

59

"dead" in 5:27 more frequently means "ravished" or "despoiled." The translation of the end of verse 27 really should read "at her feet he sank, he fell, where he sank there he fell, despoiled." The singer thus points out that Sisera, the would-be despoiler of women, is despoiled by a woman. And the mother who expects to gain spoils from her son's violence loses both the spoils and the son.

The song ends with a wish that all the enemies of the LORD will perish in an equally fitting manner (5:31).

Dimension 3:
What Does the Bible Mean to Us?

What makes an action or a person praiseworthy? There is no comment in the prose story on the rightness or the wrongness of Jael's behavior. The narrator in Judges 4 describes what Jael does without telling us whether God approves or disapproves of her actions. But in the song of victory that follows, Deborah and Barak say, "Most blessed of women be Jael, the wife of Heber the Kenite, of tent-dwelling women most blessed" (5:24).

According to the prose narrative, Jael goes out of her way to offer hospitality to someone with whom her clan is at peace. She invites him into her tent, gives him milk to drink and a place to hide and to sleep. In the prose story she is even said to cover Sisera up in a protective manner. The usual codes of social behavior in the ancient world would require Jael to honor her husband's truce with Jabin.

Is Jael's Action Justifiable?
Hospitality in Jael's social world would require a host or hostess to protect anyone to whom food and shelter had been offered. Instead, she pounds a tent stake through the head of her guest, who is also her husband's treaty partner.

Jael either does not feel bound by the usual codes of behavior in her world or she chooses to disregard them. Like Ehud in Judges 3:15-25, Jael uses trickery and deceit to overcome an enemy. Both the story of Ehud of Judges 3 and the story of Jael in Judges 4–5 raise questions about how the people of God act in situations of crisis. Is this kind of behavior justifiable in certain extreme circumstances? Does the end (the death of an oppressor) justify the means by which that end was accomplished?

The story of Jael suggests that kinship ties, political alliances, and the ordinary codes of social behavior sometimes have to be broken in order to set God's people free.

What is the right thing for the faithful to do when the normal rules of acceptable behavior conflict

60

with the need of the oppressed to free themselves from oppression? The story of Jael suggests that kinship ties, political alliances, and the ordinary codes of social behavior sometimes have to be broken in order to set God's people free.

Shattering Our Expectations

The central theme in all of the stories of the Judges is the theme of reversals. The Book of Judges seems determined to challenge all our stereotypes and to reverse all our expectations. Previous experience with the social and religious traditions of Israel leads us to expect a hero rather than a heroine as an agent of God's salvation. But the words and deeds of women make up the beginning, the middle, and the end of the story told in Judges 4–5.

At the beginning of the story, we meet Deborah who is either "the wife of Lappidoth" or "a spirited woman" (the Hebrew could be read either way). As a judge she settles disputes for the people of Israel. As a prophet she transmits the word of God to Barak and his troops. Her presence is needed to reassure Barak in the midst of the battle. Together with Barak, Deborah composes and sings a significant victory hymn.

> The traditions of Israel lead us to expect a hero rather than a heroine as an agent of God's salvation. So we do not expect a woman to deliver Israel from oppression. Nor do we do expect a foreigner to risk her standing in her own community in order to free another nation from oppression. The stories in Judges tell us that God is full of surprises when it comes to selecting people to set other people free.

At the end of the story we catch a glimpse of Sisera's mother, who seems to be Deborah's opposite in every way. Her image is the traditional image of a woman in Canaan, looking out through the window of her house. While Deborah is a mother in Israel, the woman at the window is the mother of Israel's enemy. Deborah accompanies the commander of Israel's forces to the scene of battle. Sisera's mother waits at home for the commander of the Canaanite forces to return victorious. One mother will celebrate and the other will mourn the outcome of this conflict.

But the images of Deborah and of Sisera's mother fade into the background when Jael enters the picture. It is Jael, the wife of Heber the Kenite, whose actions make up the center of the story.

Unlike the Israelites, who have begun to build permanent homes in the land, Jael and her clan live in tents on the fringes of the settled communities. The Kenites are tinkers and shepherds. They wander from place to place, repairing tools and weapons and looking for grass to feed their sheep and goats.

We are told that Jael and her clan are at peace with Jabin. Sisera does not threaten Jael or her family's existence. Thus we do not expect Jael to go out of her way to rid the world of Sisera. We expect Jael to abide by the treaty and the hospitality customs of the culture in which she lives. We do not expect a foreigner to risk her standing in her own community in order to free another nation from oppression.

As the story opens, we do not expect a woman to deliver Israel from oppression. But our expectations change when Deborah warns Barak that "the LORD will sell Sisera into the hand of a woman" (4:9). At that point we would assume that Deborah (who is already a proven prophet and judge in Israel) will be the chosen one. Instead we find it is a seemingly unqualified outsider who delivers the Israelites from their distress.

In a war story we expect the commanders of the armies to be bold and brave. But Barak refuses to lead the troops out alone, and Sisera flees the battle scene and cowers in a tent while his soldiers are being slaughtered. We expect all the tribes of Israel to come to the aid of Naphtali and Zebulun. But the singers who reflect back on the events of the day emphasize that a woman who is an outsider (both by birth and behavior) saved the day for the people of God. While some of the insiders in Israel play it safe and stay out of the fight, Israel's salvation comes from an unexpected quarter.

The Book of Judges upsets our stereotyped ideas about who is qualified to become an agent of God's salvation. The stories in Judges tell us that God is full of surprises when it comes to selecting people to set other people free.

Dimension 4:
A Daily Bible Journey Plan

> *Day 1:* Judges 4:1-16
>
> *Day 2:* Judges 4:17–5:5
>
> *Day 3:* Judges 5:6-18
>
> *Day 4:* Judges 5:19-31
>
> *Day 5:* Judges 6:1-18
>
> *Day 6:* Judges 6:19-32
>
> *Day 7:* Judges 6:33–7:8

Testing: One, Two, Three

What to Watch For

The story of Gideon will be told in greater detail than any of the previous judge stories. We will find that when he is called to become a deliverer, Gideon has no confidence in that call. We will learn how the Israelite army is reduced to a very small size, how Gideon's doubts are finally put to rest, and how the Midianites are tricked into a panicky retreat. We will learn that the Israelites offer to make Gideon their king. Gideon will refuse, on the grounds that the LORD is king over Israel. Notice how often Gideon's lack of confidence is described. He needs signs to prove to himself that God's word can be trusted.

Read all of Gideon's story in Judges 6–8.

Dimension 1: What Does the Bible Say?

1. List the various ways Gideon tries to reassure himself that he has been called to deliver Israel from the power of Midian.

Repeatedly asking the Lord for a sign
Fleece wet then dry
Lord to wait while he fixed food

63

2. Why does God want to reduce the number of Israelites involved in the battle with Midian?

So there can be no doubt the victory was the Lord's

3. What enables Gideon and his small band to rout the whole Midianite army? *The Midianites were expecting to be defeated fought against themselves then ran*

Dimension 2:
What Does the Bible Mean?

The story of Gideon in Judges 6–8 could be staged as a play in three acts, with three scenes in each act. The prologue, before the curtain rises, presents a historical summary of conditions leading up to the call of Gideon.

GIDEON: THE PLAY

Prologue: The Cycle of History (6:1-10)
Act 1: Gideon chosen to deliver Israel (6:11-40).

Scene 1 (6:11-24):	Gideon is called, doubts the call.
Scene 2 (6:25-35):	Gideon overthrows a pagan altar.
Scene 3 (6:36-40):	Gideon looks for signs with fleece.

Acts 2: Encounter between Midian and Israel (7:1-25).

Scene 1 (7:1-8):	Israel's forces reduced to three hundred.
Scene 2 (7:9-14):	Gideon seeks reassurance again.
Scene 3 (7:15-25):	The Midianites panic and scatter.

Acts 3: Ridding the land of its oppressors (8:4-35).

Scene 1 (8:4-21):	Midianite kings pursued and killed.
Scene 2 (8:22-28):	People offer to make Gideon king.
Scene 3 (8:29-35):	Israelites fall back into sin.

The word translated *angel* in the opening scene really means "messenger" in Hebrew. The translators probably assumed that the only messengers of the LORD are what we traditionally think of as angels. The messenger of the LORD represents the presence of the LORD; the messenger is interchangeable with the LORD's own self. Thus in 6:14 and 16 it is no longer the messenger, but the LORD who speaks directly to Gideon. In 6:20-22 the messenger is back, but in 6:23 it is the LORD who speaks a word of peace.

When God Calls

Judges 6:11-17 is a "call story." Old Testament stories about a person's call to God's service follow a recognizable pattern. Persons who are called usually resist the call when it first comes. They give reasons why they do not consider themselves qualified. They try to avoid the service God demands of them (compare Judges 6:15 with Exodus 4:10 and Jeremiah 1:6). God's answer is always the same. God assures those who are called that they will be able to do what needs to be done. How can one be sure? Because "I will be with you" (Judges 6:16; Exodus 4;12; Jeremiah 1:8). The stories that follow in Judges 6–8 indicate that Gideon is not showing false modesty. In truth he is not a likely candidate for the task of delivering Israel. The storyteller might even have intended to evoke laughter from the audience when the messenger calls Gideon a "mighty warrior" in 6:12. Gideon's actions in the following scenes certainly show him to be more timid than mighty. Even the LORD's call for Gideon to go "in this might of yours and deliver Israel from the hand of Midian" (6:14) may have a tongue-in-cheek quality, given what we know about Gideon's later behavior.

> Persons who are called by God usually resist the call when it first comes. They give reasons why they do not consider themselves qualified. They try to avoid the service God demands of them. God's answer is always the same. God assures those who are called that they will be able to do what needs to be done. How can one be sure? Because "I will be with you."

All of the Gideon stories revolve around the themes of testing and power. In Judges 2:22, we were told that the LORD let a number of foreign nations remain in the Promised Land in order to test Israel's faithfulness. But in Judges 6–8, Gideon tests the reliability of his call (6:17). He sets up two tests involving fleece and dew to see if he has understood the LORD's promises correctly (6:36-40). God in turn sets up a water test to reduce the number of Israelites prepared to face the armies of Midian (7:1-8). But in the end Israel fails the most important test of all (8:33-34).

Power and the Hand

The theme of power enters the story in 6:1 and continues through every scene. The Hebrew word *yad*, meaning "hand" or "power," occurs twenty-six times in Chapters 6–8. It is used even more frequently here than in the Ehud story. By concentrating on the term *hand/power* the story encourages its audience to consider the origins and the nature of power. What kind of power really matters? Who has the only kind of power that matters? By whose hand (or by whose power) is Israel delivered?

Gideon himself knows that he is not the ideal man of power (6:15). And while the story of his call begins and ends with the assurance that the LORD is and will be with him (6:12, 16), Gideon doubts the truth of this affirmation. So in 6:19-21, he asks for a sign to help convince himself that this word of assurance does indeed come from God. The power of the LORD to consume Gideon's offering persuades him that he has indeed spoken with the messenger of the LORD (6:22). But then the LORD asks Gideon to destroy an altar his own family has put up to worship Baal and Asherah. He does so, but he waits till night "because he was too afraid of his family and the townspeople to do it by day" (6:27). (The word translated "sacred pole" in the NRSV of this story is the Hebrew word *asherah*.)

> Gideon's story encourages its audiences to consider the origins and the nature of power. What kind of power really matters? Who has the only kind of power that matters? By whose hand (or by whose power) is Israel delivered?

The presence of the LORD with Gideon gave him the power to act, in spite of his normally timid inclinations. But even after the spirit of the LORD takes possession of Gideon, enabling him to call his people to arms (6:34), Gideon is full of misgivings. If the only might Gideon has is the presence of the LORD with him, will that be enough to deliver Israel? In Judges 6:36-40, Gideon asks for two more signs to bolster his courage and his faith. But even then, he is not completely convinced. On the eve of the battle, after the LORD has again said, "I have given it into your hand" (7:9), Gideon's fear remains. When he overhears words interpreting the dream of a Midianite soldier, Gideon becomes convinced that the LORD will indeed carry the day. Recognizing the true source of power, Gideon's immediate reaction is to bow down and worship (7:15).

Who has the kind of power that matters? That question is raised when the townspeople want to kill Gideon for destroying their worship center. Gideon's father says, "if Baal is a god, let him fight for himself" (6:31). Only silence follows. Baal does not have the kind of power that matters. But, the story insists, neither does Israel have that kind of power unless God is with them.

In Judges 7:2, the LORD acknowledges Israel's tendency to delude itself with regard to its own power. The LORD knows that the Israelites will be tempted to take the credit themselves for their own deliverance. In order to make it clear to Israel that they themselves do not have the kind of power needed to defeat their enemies, the LORD directs Gideon to reduce the army of Israel to a meager three hundred fighting men.

The Test Involving Drinking Water

The two themes of testing and power merge in 7:4-7 as the sifting of the three hundred soldiers depends upon what they do with their hands (*yad*) when they are drinking. The present state of the Hebrew text makes it impossible for us to tell exactly how the three hundred drank from the stream. Most modern translations try to make sense of the text by moving phrases around, hoping to smooth away the problems with the original text. There are basically two possible ways to understand the now-garbled text. Either the three hundred who were chosen were the best of the lot (the most faithful, the most cautious, and so forth) or they were the worst of the lot (becoming unguarded and vulnerable as they put heads down and lapped the water like dumb animals). The point of reducing the numbers remains clear in either case. When the victory is won Israel must realize that they could not have done it without the LORD's help.

All through Judges 7, the narrator emphasizes the key role the LORD plays in the defeat of Midian. There is no doubt in the narrator's mind that it is the LORD who delivers Israel. The LORD says, "I will deliver you" in 7:7 and "I have given it into your hand" in 7:9. Gideon says, "the LORD has given the army of Midian into your hand" in 7:15. Although Gideon's forces make enough noise to throw Midian into a panic, the narrator clearly specifies that "the LORD set every man's sword against his fellow" (7:22).

> When the victory is won Israel must realize that they could not have done it without the LORD's help.

The narrator tells us that the evidence was clear. Everyone should have realized who had the power that mattered in this struggle. Even a Midianite soldier knew that God had given Midian into Gideon's hand (7:14). But when the battle was over and the dust of the chase had settled, the people of Israel credited Gideon (not the LORD) with the victory (8:22)!

Gideon After the Victory

The people offer the kingship to Gideon. Gideon's refusal seems at first to be a statement of faith: "I will not rule over you, and my son will not rule over you; the LORD will rule over you." But Gideon's next request casts a shadow over his motives. Gideon asks for a share of the gold the Israelites have taken as spoils from the Midianites. He makes the gold into an ephod, and puts it in his hometown, where "all Israel prostituted themselves to it."

The ephod is first mentioned in Exodus 28:6-14 and 39:2-7. There it seems to have been an outer garment reserved for the use of the high priest. It was woven with linen and golden threads and had a pocket in which the sacred lots were kept. The ephod seems to have been used to consult with the LORD. When an answer was required from God, the ephod was brought out so the sacred lots could be cast from the special pocket (see 1 Samuel 23:9-12). Thus Gideon refuses to accept royal power but asks for the power to be certain in matters of faith. Gideon's quest for certainty eventually becomes a snare to him and to his family. The hero who began to liberate his people by pulling down one set of idols ends up leading his people into another form of idolatry because of his inability to believe that the LORD was truly with him.

Dimension 3: What Does the Bible Mean to Us?

As the Gideon story opens, God's patience with Israel seems to be wearing thin. In Judges 3:9, 3:15, and 4:3, the cry of the people prompts God to send a deliverer without delay. But in 6:7-10, God sends a prophet in response to the people's cry. The prophet reminds Israel that they have to take some responsibility on themselves for the present state of their affairs.

When the messenger of the LORD appears to Gideon and says, "The LORD is with you," Gideon is not immediately convinced. Gideon has heard all of the old, old stories about God's wonderful deeds in other times and places (6:13), but he has not seen any of these wonders performed in his own lifetime.

Is Success Sure When the LORD Is With Us?

What does it mean for the LORD to be with us? Does the presence of the LORD with us banish our feelings of inadequacy? Does the presence of the LORD with us guarantee our success in every endeavor?

So Gideon finds the angel's affirmation hard to believe. "But sir," he protests, "if the LORD is with us, why then has all this happened to us?" (6:13).

Gideon's question still bothers many people of faith today. What does it mean for the LORD to be with us? Does the presence of the LORD with us banish our feelings of inadequacy? Does the presence of the LORD with us guarantee our success in every endeavor?

Gideon thought that if the LORD was with Israel they would not have fallen into the oppressive hands of Midian. But the historians of Israel thought otherwise. In their account of Israel's failure to occupy the Promised Land, the historians noted that "the LORD was with Judah . . . but [Judah] could not drive out the inhabitants of the plain, because they had chariots of iron" (1:19). The historians apparently believed that God's presence with Israel set up the possibility for success but did not guarantee it.

Neither did they think that the presence of God with Israel necessarily filled Israel with confidence. The historians noted that "the LORD was with" the house of Joseph, but the Joseph tribes still felt the need to rely on spies and traitors to conquer Bethel (Judges 1:22-25).

Gideon's insecure faith is a constant theme in Judges 6–8. The messenger assured Gideon that the LORD was with him. But Gideon still felt the need to set up test after test to bolster his confidence in his ability to do what God called him to do. Gideon was not at all sure that the power of God would be able to deliver Israel by the hand of a much-less-than-powerful man like himself.

Do Our Doubts Make God Withdraw the Call?

Sometimes we assume that our doubts or our lack of faith makes us ineligible to serve the LORD in significant ways. But it is clear that a certain amount of doubt does not disqualify Gideon in God's eyes. Gideon has persistent feelings of inadequacy and fear. But the LORD neither ridicules Gideon nor rejects him on account of his fears. Instead it seems that the LORD is remarkably patient with Gideon, giving him sign after sign to bolster his courage.

There comes a point, however, when the evidence of God's presence with Gideon becomes overwhelming. It is at this point (after the victory over the Midianites has been accomplished) that Gideon's continuing quest for certainty in matters of faith becomes a snare to him and his family (8:27). The ephod may have seemed to offer security for Gideon. He and his fellow Israelites may have thought they could trust the power of the ephod to guide their lives. But the historian saw their dependence on anything other than the LORD in a negative light. In the historian's eyes "all Israel prostituted themselves" to the ephod "and it became a snare to Gideon and to his family."

The Gideon story begins and ends with Israel's failure to recognize whose hand it is that rescues them from their enemies all around (6:10; 8:34). In this story full of testing motifs, it is clear that Israel failed the ultimate test: they "did not remember the LORD their God who had rescued them from the hand [power] of all their enemies on every side" (8:34). Instead, they "prostituted themselves" to the ephod that Gideon made to help his unbelief; and they "prostituted themselves with the Baals, making Baal-berith their god" (8:33).

> The potential for victory is present when the LORD is with Israel, with Gideon, or with us; but that victory depends in part on our own participation in the struggle.

Competing Powers Today

Various powers compete for our ultimate loyalties today just as they did in Gideon's time. And the people of God alive today continue to misindentify the sources of their security.

In Judges 6–8, our ancestors in the faith tell us (in story form) that the potential for victory is present when the LORD is with Israel, with Gideon, or with us; but that victory depends in part on our own participation in the struggle.

The Gideon story teaches us a double-edged lesson. On the one hand, our own participation, inept as it may be, is required in order for us to be delivered from the consequences of our sins. On the other hand, we have to remember that without God neither Israel nor any of us can be delivered from the consequences of our sin. When the victory is won we must remember to give the credit to God.

On the one hand, God does not choose to act alone. God requires us to participate in our own escape from oppression. On the other hand, God wants us to recognize that we could not have done it alone. We could not have triumphed except for the presence of God with us in every endeavor.

The Gideon stories ask us to consider what kind of power really matters. They challenge us to correctly identify the source of that power. They tell us not to underestimate what the power of God with us can do. And they remind us that total certainty is not possible in matters of faith. God is willing to allow us a great deal of room for doubt. But an unending quest for physical proofs of the presence of God with us soon becomes idolatry.

Dimension 4:
A Daily Bible Journey Plan

Day 1: Judges 7:9-25

Day 2: Judges 8:1-12

Day 3: Judges 8:13-28

Day 4: Judges 8:29–9:6

Day 5: Judges 9:7-21

Day 6: Judges 9:22-41

Day 7: Judges 9:42-57

Judges 10–12

PARENTAL DISCRETION ADVISED

What to Watch For

If the stories in Judges were made into a movie or television series, they would probably need to be accompanied by a warning—"For Mature Audiences Only" or "Parental Discretion Advised." Graphic violence will abound. The historians of Israel will continue to document the pervasive sinfulness of Israel. Tragic stories will show that the fabric of Israel's faith is full of holes. In Chapter 11, we will meet Jephthah, a rejected child who grows up to be an insecure hero. We later meet Jephthah's unnamed daughter, who will be sacrificed in fulfillment of her father's careless vow. Read Chapters 10–12 if you have time. Be sure to read Judges 11:1-11, 29-40, and 12:1-6.

Dimension 1:
What Does the Bible Say?

1. What are we told about Jephthah's background? (Judges 11:1-3)

He was the son of a prostitute
and rejected by his half brothers

2. What bargain does Jephthah make with the "elders of Gilead"? (Judges 11:4-11)

He could be the ruler if he beat the Ammonites

3. What exactly does Jephthah vow to do? What does he ask in return? Does God agree to the bargain? (Judges 11:29-32)

Sacrifice whatever comes thru his door first if he beats th Ammonites

4. What is the end result of Jephthah's attempt to bargain with God? (Judges 11:34-39a)

He has to sacrifice his daughter

5. Why did the ancient quarrel between Ephraimites and Gileadites result in forty-two thousand deaths at the fords of the Jordan? (Judges 12:4-6)

Dimension 2:
What Does the Bible Mean?

At the beginning of Gideon's stories, the historical summary implied that God's patience with Israel had begun to wear thin in Gideon's time (Judges 6:7-10). Another historical summary introduces the Jephthah story and strengthens that impression. When the cycle of history is repeated in 10:6-10, there is a new twist at the end. The historian tells us that when the Israelites cried out against the oppressions of Ammon, the Lord told them, "Go and cry out to the gods whom you have chosen, let them deliver you in the time of your distress" (10:14). This time around we are told that the LORD rejects the Israelites' cry for help (10:10-14) until they actually "put away the foreign gods from among them" for a while (10:15-16).

One Man's Conflicts Without and Within
Jephthah is introduced to us as a child born out of wedlock, the result of a liaison between Gilead and a prostitute. Those who considered themselves

the legitimate heirs of Gilead drove Jephthah away from his inheritance. But in exile, the rejected child became a mighty warrior, with a band of outlaws at his command (11:3). When the burden of Ammonite oppression became unbearable to the people of Gilead, the very kinsmen who had rejected him came to beg Jephthah to lead their troops in the fight against Ammon.

There is an ironic echo between Jephthah's situation and the relationship between Israel and the LORD. Like Jephthah, the LORD has been rejected by the very people who cry to him for help. Jephthah says, as the LORD might well say to Israel, "Are you not the very ones who rejected me . . . ? So why do you come to me now when you are in trouble?" (11:7; compare 10:13-14).

> The very kinsmen who had rejected Jephthah came to beg him to lead their troops in the fight against Ammon. Like Jephthah, the LORD has been rejected by the very people who cry to him for help.

The elders of Gilead first offer to make Jephthah commander of their military forces, but he bargains with them for a greater reward. They agree to his conditions. If the LORD gives him victory over the Ammonites, Jephthah will become the head or chief over all the inhabitants of Gilead.

A Judge the LORD Did Not Call

Unlike previous judges, Jephthah is not called by the LORD to deliver Israel from the power of its enemies. Instead, a human delegation chooses him, and "the people made him head and commander over them" (11:11a). We have to wait until 11:29 before we are told that "the spirit of the LORD came upon Jephthah," just as it had come before upon Othniel and Gideon in their times of need (3:10; 6:34).

Jephthah begins his work for Gilead with a diplomatic mission that tries to talk the king of Ammon out of fighting over disputed land (11:12-28). When diplomacy fails, war between Israel and Ammon seems inevitable. But before Jephthah begins to engage the Ammonites in battle, he tries to secure the victory for himself by making a bargain with the LORD in the form of a vow.

There are at least two ways to understand the relationship between what we are told in 11:29 and 11:30-31. One might assume that Jephthah made the vow under the influence of the Spirit. Or one might see the making of this vow as an act of doubt on Jephthah's part. If the presence of the LORD with Jephthah was enough to ensure the successful outcome of the battle, then the vow is a mark of unfaith. Jephthah is so concerned with achieving his

> Jephthah is so concerned with becoming ruler of Gilead that he feels the need to bargain with God as well as with the elders.

73

goals (becoming head of Gilead) that he feels the need to bargain with God as well as with the elders of Gilead.

The vow itself is ambiguously worded. Jephthah promises to slaughter and burn whoever or whatever comes out of his house to meet him. The Hebrew word, meaning "that which comes out," can refer to either a person or a thing. Did Jephthah know that he was risking his daughter's life when he made the vow? The narrator does not say. The dismay Jephthah expresses when his daughter comes out to meet him implies that he did not foresee this possible consequence of his words. But it was not unknown for women to greet returning victors with music and dancing (Exodus 15:19-21; 1 Samuel 18:6-7).

Jephthah may have thought that the LORD would control the movements of his household, that the LORD would choose who or what would be the victim for the sacrifice Jephthah promised to make.

Blame the Victim!

If Jephthah thought the LORD had chosen his daughter, we might expect him to cry out to the LORD in anguish or protest. Instead, Jephthah's grief is self-centered. He blames his daughter for being the cause of his pain (11:35). She, however, refuses to take the blame for her father's actions. She reminds him that he was the one who made the vow and set the terms for completing it (11:36). She accepts the suffering imposed on her by her father's unfaithfulness, but she will not allow him to escape the burden of responsibility for his own actions.

Human sacrifice may have played a part in the religious practices of other ancient Near Eastern cultures. According to 2 Kings 3:27, Mesha king of Moab "took his firstborn son who was to succeed him, and offered him as a burnt offering on the wall" of the fortress that was being attacked by Israel. Other Old Testament texts imply that the Ammonites burned children as sacrifices to the god Molech. Thus it seems that Jephthah offered to give the LORD an Ammonite type of sacrificial offering in return for an Ammonite defeat!

Human sacrifice was universally condemned by the laws and the prophets in Israel. Firstborn animals were given to God as sacrificial offerings. But firstborn children were to be "redeemed" by substituting an animal for the child.

But human sacrifice was universally condemned by the laws and the prophets in Israel. The cultic codes of Israel did ask people to dedicate all firstborn male creatures to God ("all that first opens the womb is mine," Exodus 34:19). Firstborn animals were given to God as sacrificial offerings. But firstborn children were to be "redeemed" by substituting an animal for the child (Exodus 13:13-15). Other nations might "burn their sons and daughters in the fire to their gods," but the LORD considered this practice "an abhorrent thing" (Deuteronomy 12:29-32).

The characters in this story seem to assume that God might sometimes require (or at least accept) human sacrifices. They seem to assume that a father has the right to slaughter his own child in return for favors from God. No one in the story specifically condemns the father for his actions. However, those who were responsible for including the Jephthah story in the Book of Judges did not approve of the assumptions of the persons in the story. The historians of Israel continually remind us that the society described in the Jephthah story is a sinful society. The story's emphasis on the daughter's virginity may have something to do with her eligibility as a potential sacrifice. But the daughter's request for time to bewail her unmarried status probably stems from ancient Israelite beliefs about the importance of having children to carry on one's name. In Old Testament times people were thought to live on after death only through their off-spring. A person had to have children in order to achieve some small degree of immortality. It was thought that a childless man or woman had no one to carry his or her memory into the future. But the conclusion to this story challenges that belief. Jephthah's daughter was remembered in spite of her childlessness (11:40).

There is a kind of ironic justice implied in this conclusion. Jephthah's daughter's memory lived on. The women of Israel commemorated her death in an annual ritual (11:40). But her father's name died when she did. Since she was his only child, her sacrifice brought about the end of Jephthah's line of descent.

Jephthah had bargained with both the elders of Gilead and with God, in order to attain power and glory. Jephthah wanted to make sure his own role in the victory would be recognized and rewarded.

When Poor Pronunciation Meant Death

In Judges 12, the "men of Ephraim" are also engaged in a search for glory. They complain because they have missed participating in the victory over Ammon. A similar story was told in Judges 8, where the Ephraimites complained that Gideon had not called them into the fight against Midian. In the Gideon story, we were told that the LORD had reduced Gideon's army to a mere three hundred men, so that Israel would not be able to say, "My own hand has delivered me" (Judges 7:2). The Ephraimite attitude seems to typify the reaction the LORD had hoped to avoid.

Gideon used flattery to soothe the Ephraimites' wounded pride (Judges 8:2-3). But the troops under Jephthah's command were apparently enraged by the Ephraimites' slurs against their ancestry (12:4). Gilead was a minority group within Manasseh. Both Ephraim and Manasseh traced their parentage back to Joseph. The Ephraimites mock the Gileadites, calling them the rejects or the dregs (NRSV says "fugitives") of the tribe. In retaliation the Gileadites devise a pronunciation test against the Ephraimites.

Those who fail the test become rejects (fugitives) at the fords of the Jordan (12:6).

The word translated *ford* is based on the root word meaning "cross over." The Hebrew word for crossing occurs six times in six verses in Judges 12:1-6. In Joshua 3–4, crossing over was an event full of promise, leading to a new life in a new land. Now, only a few generations later, crossing over the Jordan leads to the death of forty-two thousand Ephraimites at the hands of their own kin. Sin has rotted the fibers of Israel's life in the Promised Land.

Dimension 3: What Does the Bible Mean to Us?

Like many other biblical narratives, the Jephthah story is open to a wide variety of interpretations. There are numerous gaps or silences in the text. They have to be filled in the readers' imaginations in order for us to make sense out of the story.

What the Narrator Leaves to Us

For instance, the narrator merely reports the making of the vow, without commenting on the rightness or the wrongness of such an action. It is up to the reader to decide whether this is an act of faith or an act of doubt.

> Is Jephthah's vow an act of faith or an act of doubt? What would have happened if Jephthah had broken the vow once it was made?

The narrator does not tell us whether the LORD was impressed by or disgusted by Jephthah's attempt to control the outcome of the battle. We are not told whether the LORD wanted Jephthah's to make such a sacrifice or to keep such a vow once it had been made. We do not hear any response from God agreeing to Jephthah's offer. We are merely told that the vow has terrible consequences.

Whenever possible, the filling in of narrative silences should take into account other biblical texts that consider the same issues. Because the Jephthah narrative is selectively silent, we are left to wonder whether it is true that this vow, once made, really could not have been broken. We are not told what might have happened if Jephthah had refused to follow through with his promise.

We can find other biblical texts that emphasize the importance of fulfilling vows once they are made. But the Scriptures also indicate that the making of vows is not necessary: "If you refrain from vowing you will not incur guilt" (Deuteronomy 23:22). Other texts urge people to be very careful about making vows: "Do not let your mouth lead you into sin" (Ecclesiastes 5:4-6). The reader might thus conclude with some degree of confidence that Jephthah's vow was not necessary and that Jephthah had indeed allowed his mouth to lead him into sin.

The way each community of faith fills in the silences in the story depends essentially on the presuppositions that community brings to its readings of the text. We all fill in the silences based on our prior beliefs about God and the world.

Everyone comes to the reading of a biblical narrative with some preconceived notions. We come to the Jephthah story already prepared to believe certain things about God. We already have ideas about how God does or does not act in relation to humankind. And we draw conclusions about what the text does not say based on these ideas that we bring with us to the reading of the text.

Does a Vow Mean Trust or Doubt?

When we find (for example) that the narrator does not say whether the making of the vow had anything to do with the victory over Ammon, we draw our own conclusions. We decide whether we think the victory came as a result of the vow or in spite of it.

God's presence and God's help is either given freely to us or not at all. God does not make bargains with us. God cannot be bought with promises for future sacrifices on our part. This interpretation sees Jephthah's vow as an act of unfaith. The vow indicates that Jephthah either has failed to recognize the presence of the spirit of the LORD with him or does not trust in the power of the LORD to bring about the victory.

> If seeing ourselves and our own sins reflected in the biblical text leads us to repentance, then the texts will have functioned as agents of redemption for us.

The stories in Judges 10–12 may seem on a superficial level to have little redemptive value. But they can become instruments of redemption for us if we allow ourselves to see how our own behavior sometimes mirrors the behavior of the characters in the story. If seeing ourselves and our own sins reflected in the biblical text leads us to repentance, then the texts will have functioned as agents of redemption for us.

Like Jephthah we also can fail either to recognize or to trust in the power of the presence of the LORD. Like Jephthah many of us are unable to believe that the presence of the LORD alone is enough to overcome that which oppresses us. Like Jephthah, many of us seek to control rather than to trust the power of God. And like Jephthah many of us put our children's lives on the line in our attempts to gain power and glory for ourselves.

Sacrificing Daughters and Sons Today

Most of us would agree that child sacrifice is an abhorrent practice. But many common practices in the modern world have the same result. In the story, Jephthah attempts to guarantee his future but he ends up sacrificing it instead.

Can the Jephthah story function redemptively in our own lives? We might let it prompt us to investigate the ways our present actions may eventually cut off our own and our children's futures. Consider for example, whether our generation's disregard for the health of the environment may be as deadly a gamble with our children's lives as the gamble Jephthah made with his daughter's life. When we put the future of our natural environment in jeopardy in order to satisfy our present needs or wants, are we not sacrificing our own children as surely as Jephthah did? The Jephthah story begins and ends with rejection and rivalry within the family of God. The LORD is rejected by Israel (10:13). Jephthah is rejected by his Gileadite brothers (11:2). The Gileadites are rejected by their Ephraimite kin (12:4). Entry into the Promised Land did not fill the people of God with a durable faith. And the erosion of faith can have tragic consequences.

> When we put the future of our natural environment in jeopardy in order to satisfy our present needs or wants, are we not sacrificing our own children as surely as Jephthah did?

In Judges 11:4-11, we are told that Jephthah bargained with those who rejected him in order to attain a position of power over them. We are told that the Gileadites slaughtered those who rejected them (12:5-6). But the narrator skillfully leaves us wondering at the end: What will eventually happen to those who continue to reject the L?

A DEATH SENTENCE IN A WORD

At the fords on the Jordan river the men of Gilead stopped each passer-by. "Whenever one of the fugitives from Ephraim said, 'Let me go over,' the men of Gilead would say to him . . . 'Say Shibboleth' " (Judges 12:5-6). Evidently the Ephraimites could not pronounce "sh." They said "sibboleth" instead. That mispronunciation trapped them and became a sentence of death. Any other word with "sh" would have worked just as well. Our dictionaries tell us the word *shibboleth* has a political meaning today. A shibboleth is a word or slogan that has become code language identifying a particular group or party. Such an expression "is often retained long after its original and vital meaning has been exhausted. In political campaigns the shibboleths are numerous and often meaningless, but serve to indicate a threat or an appeal which will have some vote-getting power" (*The Interpreter's Bible*, volume 2; Abingdon, 1953; page 774).

Day 1: Judges 10:1-16

Day 2: Judges 10:17–11:11

Day 3: Judges 11:12-28

Day 4: Judges 11:29-40

Day 5: Judges 12:1-15

Day 6: Judges 13:1-14

Day 7: Judges 13:15-25

Prepare Devotion

Judges 13–16

10

A Nazirite to God from Birth?

What to Watch For

Samson's birth story in Judges 13 may lead you to hope that from the last of the deliverer-judges a great deal will be expected. An angel will tell Samson's mother that her son is to be "a nazirite," consecrated to God from birth (13:5). Nazirites were expected to lead an exemplary life in Israel (see Numbers 6:1-21). But as we read Judges 14–16, we will find that each of Samson's adventures begins with his search for instant sexual gratification (14:1; 15:1; 16:1, 4). He lusts after foreign women, members of uncircumcised nations, prostitutes, and idol-worshipers. His wanton and often foolish behavior will continually lead him into danger and result eventually in his death. Other judges have led the rest of the Israelites in battle, but Samson will insist on one-man shows. He will fight Israel's enemies all alone.

In Judges 13–16, you will find the complete story of Samson. Be sure to read at least 13:2-5, 14:1-3, and 16:4-31. (You may not want to miss Samson's riddle in 14:5-20 or the donkey's jawbone in 15:14-17.)

Dimension 1: What Does the Bible Say?

1. Compare Judges 13:4-5 and Numbers 6:1-8. What specific things should a nazirite avoid?

2. How is the story of Samson and the lion (in 14:5-9) tied into the story of Samson's riddle (14:12-17)?

3. When "the spirit of the LORD rushed on him" (twice in Chapter 14 and once in Chapter 15), how did Samson react?

4. Is Samson at any time successful in convincing other Israelites to follow him into battle?

Dimension 2:
What Does the Bible Mean?

We saw on pages 48–49 how the history of the Israelites followed a cycle again and again in the Book of Judges. Alas, by the time of Samson the cycle of history is reduced to a single verse in 13:1, with no mention of repentance on Israel's part. Until this point we have had little mention of the Philistines, a powerful and treacherous enemy.

Understanding the Philistines
The Philistines were one of the "Sea Peoples" (from the Aegean area) who began to migrate into the Eastern Mediterranean area around 1200 B.C. Stone carvings found in Egypt commemorate a victory by Pharaoh Rameses III over the Sea Peoples, giving us a good idea of what the Philistines looked like, what they wore into battle, and what weapons they used.

The Philistines built a confederation of city-states in the Mediterranean coastal plains of Canaan and became the most powerful force in this corner of the world between 1150 and 1000 B.C. Both Shamgar (Judges 3:31) and Samson were pitted against the Philistines in the era of the judges, but Philistine oppression continued to be a problem in Samuel's time (1 Samuel 4). It was pressure from the Philistines that led the people to demand a king like other nations (1 Samuel 7). The king chosen was Saul, who was engaged in war with the Philistines for his entire career (1 Samuel 13–31). David was the king who finally defeated the Philistines, making Israel the leading power in Canaan around 1000 B.C. The modern name *Palestine* comes from the Greek word meaning the "land of the Philistines."

Samson Was No Samuel!

In Judges 13, we have an intentionally humorous, tongue-in-cheek introduction to the parents of a hero whose morals will leave a great deal to be desired.

> The story of Samson's dedication heightens the irony of his misbehavior. Israelite audiences probably laughed at the idea that he, of all people, had been dedicated to God from his mother's womb!

Samson's birth story is a parody of a story yet to come, that of Samuel's birth (1 Samuel 1). Samson and Samuel are both said to "judge" Israel. They and their careers are completely opposite in character. Samuel is an ideal theological hero. His strength comes from his moral and religious dedication. But Samson is a lusty rogue, whose adventures have self-serving rather than religious or political foundations. He does not fight to defend either his own tribe (Dan) or Israel as a whole. Instead his raids against the Philistines are meant to avenge personal insults and injuries.

Samson's behavior would have been considered bad enough in an ordinary Israelite. But an ancient audience would have been even more shocked to think that one who had been dedicated from birth to God's service had acted the way Samson did. The story of his nazirite dedication heightens the irony of Samson's behavior. Israelite audiences probably laughed at the idea that he, of all people, had been dedicated to God from his mother's womb!

Samson's first series of adventures begins with his determination to marry a woman whose people are uncircumcised idol-worshipers. Ignoring his parents' objections, he persuades his father to arrange his betrothal. At the wedding feast, Samson challenges the thirty "companions" supplied by his bride's people to a battle of wits.

The "companions" are stumped and threaten the bride to get her to discover the answer (14:15).

An Unfair Riddle

Thus the companions cheated to win, but then so had Samson cheated in posing the riddle in the first place. The reader needs to realize what the Philistine companions could not have known: Samson is posing an unfair question. A riddle is supposed to be solvable from the clues given within it. But Samson poses a question based on circumstances known only to himself. The Philistines turn the tables on Samson. They take advantage of the clever riddler's inability to resist his bride's teasing to bring about his defeat.

When Samson realizes he has been tricked by his intended victims, he responds with an obscenely funny bellow of rage against his wife (14:18b). He takes revenge by slaughtering and robbing thirty of the winners' fellow-countrymen in order to pay off his losses.

The honey-in-the-carcass story adds a note of infamy to Samson's behavior in Judges 14. Anything that had touched a dead carcass should have been considered unclean (Leviticus 5:2; 11:24-38). Both Samson and his mother were supposed to avoid touching or eating anything unclean (Judges 13:7, 14). But Samson eats from a honeycomb that is unclean (because it has touched a dead body) and gives some of the unclean honey to his mother without telling her where it came from.

Exaggerated Humor to Delight Rude Listeners

The adventures in Judges 14–15, which begin with the wedding feast and end on Jawbone hill, sound more like locker-room tales than heroic legends. The tone throughout is light-heartedly obscene. Samson's victory song in 15:16 is a play on words that would be better translated, "With the jawbone of an ass, I made bloody asses of them all." Both the numbers used in Judges 15 (three hundred foxes, three thousand men of Judah, a thousand men slain with a fresh jawbone) and the bizarre character of Samson's exploits indicate that these stories owe more to the imagination of the narrator than to factual record.

Judges 16:1-3 may have been told sheerly to poke fun at the Philistines. Samson's sexual appetites again lead him into Philistine territory. His enemies in Gaza set a trap for him that he cleverly springs. Then Samson adds the jest of insult to their failure by carrying off the gates within which they had hoped to ensnare him. The gates of a city like Gaza would have been built of massive blocks of stone. To carry them from Gaza to the heights of Hebron would involve a rather fantastic journey of about forty miles, with an ascent of over three thousand feet. The exaggerations in the story are meant to be funny, to make the Philistines look puny in comparison to Samson.

Samson's own weaknesses accomplish what the Philistines themselves could not— his defeat.

In the Delilah story (Judges 16:4-22), Samson's own weaknesses accomplish what the Philistines themselves could not. Samson's contempt for the Philistines and his repeated success in fooling them and in resisting Delilah's attempts to ensnare him lead him into overconfidence. He foolishly lowers his guard in the face of Delilah's teasing and falls victim to her superior wiles. Delilah might be called the Philistine equivalent of Jael

(Judges 4–5). Although Delilah is not on Israel's side, like Jael she breaks the hospitality code to lure a powerful enemy to his death.

At the end of the story, Samson is returned to Gaza, the scene of his former victory, in abject defeat (Judges 16:21). But as the Philistines gloat over their captive, the tables are turned once more and the chapter ends as it began, with Samson triumphant in Gaza, the stronghold of the enemy.

Dimension 3: What Does the Bible Mean to Us?

Samson clearly did not ask to be a nazirite, nor did he ever agree to abide by the nazirite rules. They are expectations that seem to have been imposed upon him by God and by his family. Samson seems to go out of his way to break as many of the restrictions imposed on him at birth as he can, even though he knows that they are the ultimate source of his strength (16:17).

Strength and Weakness in a Lethal Combination

Physical strength is an important part of Samson's image. He is never said to fall victim to superior strength alone. Samson's failures are all ultimately due to his foolishness. He lacks moral rather than physical stamina.

The literature of many peoples features characters somewhat like Samson. They are usually identified as "tricksters." Like many other trickster figures, Samson is at times admirably clever and at other times incredibly stupid. He poses an ingenious riddle but is duped into giving away its solution. He cleverly avoids falling into one trap in Gaza, then stupidly steps right into another.

The narrator tells us that Samson's actions fit somehow into the LORD's intentions. According to 14:4, the LORD "was seeking a pretext to act against the Philistines." But Samson himself never seems aware that he is serving the LORD. When he takes outrageous forms of revenge against the Philistines, he seems to do so for his own self-centered purposes. He shows no overt willingness to work for the good of all Israel or for God.

Both ancient and modern interpreters have been puzzled and embarrassed by the self-serving nature of Samson's escapades. Most readers regard the use of deception as an acceptable means of self-defense against overwhelming odds, particularly when the retaliation seems in right proportion to the provocation. We may admire tricksters who are forced by circumstances beyond their control to resort to trickery in order to survive. We are not shocked if they use their wits to equalize the odds that are stacked against them in the story-world. But we often have more difficulty dealing with those whose tricks seem to be prompted by self-centered desires rather than a plot against the enemy.

Where Is the Value in Samson's Story?

A humorless appraisal of these stories sometimes prompts readers to try to rationalize or to justify Samson's behavior as something God ordained in order to accomplish God's mysterious purposes. Readers sometimes try to excuse Samson's actions as necessary in order to accomplish God's will.

It is probably more helpful to understand these stories as a kind of tendency wit (a form of humor that makes fun of human foibles).

As tendency wit, the Samson stories can serve two completely distinct functions. They can be used both to ridicule the Philistines and to reveal the people of God subconsciously to themselves.

> Samson's escapades provided Israelites with the occasion to have a good laugh at the enemy's expense. Such stories may have strengthened the earliest audiences in their determination to resist the Philistines.

At the most basic level, the stories in Judges 13–16 reflect a situation of tension between a relatively powerless Israel and their Philistine overlords. In 15:11, the three thousand men of Judah imply that Samson has played an unfair trick on them by stirring up the Philistines. "What have you done to us?" they indignantly demand. "Do you not know that the Philistines are rulers over us?" The stories that follow imply that the answer is "No." Neither Samson nor those who tell his stories will ever show respect to Philistine authority. Samson even conducts his amorous escapades within the very strongholds of the enemy! So in their earliest usages, the Samson stories may have functioned as resistance stories aimed against Philistine oppression. Samson's escapades provided Israelites with the occasion to have a good laugh at the enemy's expense. The telling of such stories may have strengthened the earliest audiences in their determination to resist the Philistines.

However, the Samson stories continued to function meaningfully in Israel long after the Philistines ceased to be a threat to Israelite security. In a much later period, the historians of Israel used the Samson stories to teach a timely lesson to their contemporaries.

When the historians included the Samson stories in the Book of Judges, they surrounded them with repetitive statements about Israel's sinful behavior in the period of the judges. These continual reminders served to direct the reader's attention away from the insults Samson gave to the enemy. Instead the reader was encouraged to evaluate Samson's behavior. The historians saw that Samson's wanton behavior continually led him into danger (and finally to his death). Though he managed to bring about the deaths of many Philistines, in the end Samson was unable to escape the consequence of his blatant disregard for the laws of Israel.

Israel's Choice: Samson or Samuel

Thus the ironic introduction to the Samson cycle (in Chapter 13) reminds a later audience who knew about Samuel, devoted at birth to live as a sacrifice to God, that Samson's birth could have led to a life of devotion to the LORD. Israel knows that Samuel is the hero they feel they ought to imitate. Samson is the one they most resemble. Like Samson, the people of Israel have repeatedly and foolishly fallen into the clutches of the enemy. They have repeatedly violated the covenant that was the true source of their strength.

> Like Samson, the people of Israel have repeatedly and foolishly fallen into the clutches of the enemy. They have repeatedly violated the covenant that was the true source of their strength.

Like Samson, Israel was meant to be dedicated to God from birth. But also like Samson, God's chosen people have gone whoring among the pagans once too often and have suffered the consequences.

The Samson stories can continue to have meaning for us in modern times, if we are willing to see ourselves and our own strengths and weaknesses reflected in the dynamics of the texts. A reader who identifies with Samson can laugh therapeutically at both the triumphs and the failures of the wise fool. In Samson's triumphs we can see our enemies vanquished. In his failures we can see our inner selves unmasked and exposed to therapeutic ridicule.

Dimension 4: A Daily Bible Journey Plan

Day 1: Judges 14:1-9

Day 2: Judges 14:10-20

Day 3: Judges 15:1-17

Day 4: Judges 15:18–16:9

Day 5: Judges 16:10-22

Day 6: Judges 16:23-31

Day 7: Judges 17:1-13

THEY DID WHAT WAS RIGHT IN THEIR OWN EYES

What to Watch For

The last five chapters of the Book of Judges will tell us what happened to
the covenant community of Israel when the people had no "king" (either
divine or human) to judge them. In the first part of Judges, we found the
"sight" of the LORD as the standard for evaluating Israel's behavior (3:7;
3:12; 4:1; 6:1; 10:6; 13:1). Then the Israelites will seem to decide that no
eyes are watching them other than their own. "What seems right" will be
decided by no one but them (17:6; 21:25).

Thus in Judges 17–18 the Danites will feel free to carve out a territory
for themselves and to establish an illegitimate shrine, furnished with an
idol and other religious objects stolen from one of their fellow Israelites.
Judges 19–21 will picture a society totally out of control. Be warned:
Some of these texts will speak of violence in graphic and brutal terms.
When no one (not even the LORD) is king, violence will reign supreme.
Read at least Judges 17:1-11; 18:1-29; 19:1-29; 21:25.

Dimension 1: What Does the Bible Say?

1. What does the man named Micah do with eleven hundred pieces of sil-
ver? Who does he select as a priest at his shrine? (Judges 17:1-13)

Steals from mother then returns it + makes
idol. A Levite

2. Why did the Levite from the hill country of Ephraim travel to
Bethlehem? On the return trip who was with him? Why was he unwilling
to stay overnight in the city of Jebus? (Judges 19:1-12; see also Joshua
15:63)

Went to concubines fathers
They weren't Jewish

3. Compare the Levite's public account of the event in 20:3-6 with the
same tragic incident in 19:22-29. What does the Levite add to the story
when he tells it? What does he leave out?

They wanted to kill him vs. have sex c̄ him

4. What happens to the Benjaminites when they refuse to give up the
criminals for punishment? (Judges 20:12-35)

The other tribes rise up against them

The movement of Israel's faith from the beginning of Joshua to the end of
Judges is pictured by the historians as a downhill slide. The last five chapters of Judges illustrate how far Israel has fallen into the depths of sin.

According to the historians, the people who crossed over the Jordan into
the Promised Land were a cohesive group. All Israel worked together in
Joshua's time to conquer the land. Joshua, God's chosen representative,
was their leader. But from the beginning of their history (in Joshua) until
its end (in 2 Kings 25:30) the historians have warned us not to be too opti-
mistic about Israel's future in the Promised Land.

The Downward Spiral Continues
The success or failure of Israel's endeavor depended on the people's col-
lective ability to keep the covenant they and their ancestors had made with
the ultimate owner of the land. The covenant spelled out what it meant to
do right in the eyes of God.

But the first chapter of Joshua hints at the difficulty the people of God
will have in keeping their covenant promises. Over and over again they

are urged to "be strong and courageous" in keeping the laws of the covenant (Joshua 1:7-9; see also 1:6, 18). The historians knew, from their study of the past, that it had been harder for Israel to keep the commandments than it was for them to conquer Canaan!

In Joshua 8:32-35, the historians report the process by which the laws of the LORD were handed on from one generation to another. The reading of the law was addressed to "all the assembly of Israel" including "the women, and the little ones, and the aliens who resided among them" (8:35). We read that Joshua repeatedly warned "all Israel" that if they wished to have "rest" in the land they would have to be very careful "to love the LORD your God" (23:11) and keep the provisions of the covenant. "If you transgress the covenant of the LORD your God . . . you shall perish quickly from the good land that he has given to you" (23:16).

> It was harder for Israel to keep the commandments than it was for them to conquer Canaan!

But the historians concluded that all of these warnings had been forgotten in the generation that followed Joshua (Judges 2:10). They described the entire period of history between the death of Joshua and the beginning of David's reign as an endless cycle moving from sin to punishment and back again. The activities of the judges provided only brief periods of respite. And even the behavior of the judges themselves varied from questionable to outrageous. Deborah, the possible exception to the rule, was more of a prophetess than a deliverer. The deliverance that came in Deborah's time depended on Barak and Jael, neither of whom is totally admirable.

According to the historians, none of the judges attempted to lead Israel into a more faithful lifestyle. Not one of them (not even Deborah, in her role of prophetess) tried to remind Israel of its covenant obligations.

Two Levite Antiheroes

Finally, the historians tell us in Judges 17–21, even the priests of Israel shirked their religious and moral responsibilities. The leading characters in the final chapters of Judges are identified as a "Levite" or a "priest."

The Levites were set apart in the time of Moses for the express purpose of keeping and teaching the laws of the covenant to all the future generations of Israel. But in Chapter 17, an opportunistic Levite agrees to tend a shrine dedicated to a graven image, ignoring the commandments of the covenant (Exodus 20:4; Deuteronomy 5:8; and so forth). In Judges 18, when the tribe of Dan sets out on its opportunistic quest for land, this same Levite joins them in building and staffing another idolatrous shrine as their tribal center of worship. And in Judges 19–21, it is a Levite of questionable character who sets the stage for civil war in Israel.

The final chapters in
the Book of Judges
illustrate in a stark and
terrifying manner what
can happen when indi-
viduals act as laws
unto themselves.

The final chapters in the Book of Judges have been called "texts of terror." They illustrate in a stark and terrifying manner what can happen when individuals act as laws unto themselves. The spiral of violence begins in Judges 19 with the gang rape of a woman who is identified only as the "concubine" of "a certain Levite."

The Old Testament texts sometimes reflect a society in which a man could have more than one wife (see 1 Samuel 1:1-2; 2 Samuel 5:13; and so forth). In such a family system, a concubine is a legal wife of secondary status. Even if the Levite in this story had other wives, he was bound to his concubine by custom and covenant. The woman's father is consistently referred to as the Levite's "father-in-law" (Judges 19:4-9).

The Levite and his wife stop in Gibeah, a city belonging to the tribe of Benjamin. There a fellow countryman (from the hill country of Ephraim) offers them hospitality for the night. In a scene that echoes the Sodom story in Genesis 19, a group of men surround the house in a threatening manner. The men are referred to both as Benjaminites and as "sons of beliya'al." The term *beliya'al* seems to refer either to the forces of chaos or to the underworld; so it might be translated, "the local hell-raisers." In other contexts the "son of beliya'al" are people who have no regard for either human or divine laws (see 1 Samuel 2:12).

In the NRSV the demand made by these "hell-raisers" is translated "that we may have intercourse with him." The meaning of the original Hebrew is not clear. Literally the men of Gibeah say, "Bring out the man who came into your house, that we may know him."

The word *know* is sometimes used in Hebrew as a euphemism for sexual intercourse. It appears to have that connotation in this text. But it seems that their goal is violence and humiliation more than homosexual activity. When the Levite thrusts his wife outside in order to save himself, "they wantonly raped her, and abused her all through the night until the morning" (Judges 19:25).

When the Levite gets up the next morning, ready to start out again on his journey, he shows no remorse for having abandoned his wife and no gratitude for having escaped the violence that was done to her. He is angry, however. He wants revenge. He takes the abused body of his wife and abuses it further by cutting it into twelve pieces. He sends these grue-some mementoes by messengers who spread the word to call together Israelites from every tribe. The Israelites who receive these symbols of cri-sis react with shock (Judges 19:30). However, since the story that led up to the concubine's death has not yet been told to the rest of Israel, it may be that their shock has to do with the dismemberment of her body rather than with the sin of Gibeah.

When the Levite finally tells his version of the event "in the assembly of the people of God," he says that the "lords of Gibeah" intended to kill him and that they raped his concubine until she died (Judges 20:5). He does not mention his own cowardly behavior on that occasion.

Intertribal Violence

When the Benjaminites refuse to hand the "scoundrels" of Gibeah over for punishment, the people who have gathered at Mizpah declare war against the whole tribe. The spiral of violence escalates into a civil war. In the end, we are told that only six hundred Benjaminite men escape the slaughter by fleeing to the "rock of Rimmon" (Judges 20:47).

Before long, however, the rest of the Israelites begin to regret the near-destruction of one of their fellow tribes. It now seems likely that the tribe of Benjamin will not survive unless wives can be found for the men who fled to escape the slaughter. However, there is a shortage of eligible women in Israel because the rest of the tribes had sworn at Mizpah not to let their daughters marry Benjaminite men. Two plans are approved to "solve" the problem. Both involve the use of violence (how else in these lawless times?).

Since the people of Jabesh-gilead had not come to the assembly at Mizpah (in response to the Levite's gruesome message), they had not taken the pledge regarding their daughters. The assembled Israelites thought Jabesh-gilead should be punished for not answering the call to arms. But they also thought the virgin daughters of Jabesh-gilead would make acceptable wives for the surviving men of Benjamin. Thus we are told that four hundred hapless young women who had never slept with a man were set aside as brides while their families and friends were "devoted to destruction" (Judges 21:8-12).

> When neither the LORD, nor the covenant, nor the priests, nor the judges rule in Israel, self-interest becomes the only norm of judgment.

The final villainy performed by the people who had no standards to guide them is reported in 21:15-23. The men of Benjamin who still needed wives were allowed to kidnap them from among the young women of Shiloh, as they danced in the fields during "the yearly festival of the LORD."

The final line in the Book of Judges represents the historians' answer to the question, "How could such things have happened in Israel?" The historians conclude that the decline in Israel's quality of life in the period of the judges is due to the individualization of morality. When neither the LORD, nor the covenant, nor the priests, nor the judges rule in Israel, self-interest becomes the only norm of judgment.

Gang rape, murder, dismemberment, civil war, genocide? Are you reading the Bible or the daily news? Many people prefer to hear only the good news and not the bad, to remember only the good deeds of the people of God. But the inclusion of the bad news of the past in our scriptural traditions reminds us of the possible consequences of our own present actions. The last five chapters of Judges illustrate what happens in a society in which each person has become the sole standard of his or her own morality.

Our Need to See the Ugly Side

The biblical news from the time of the judges is not all bad. The Book of Ruth, which immediately follows Judges in most English Bibles, is also set in this period of time before there was a king in Israel. In Ruth we will see that living and acting in ways that are right in the eyes of the LORD is still possible, even in terror-filled times. But we must not skip too easily over these stories of terror in our hurry to find less painful reading.

> The honesty of Judges should encourage us to consider the causes of violence and terror in our own time. We need to ask, "Is history repeating itself in my lifetime? And if so, what can I do about it?"

The historians of Israel lived and did their writing in a time of extreme crisis in their own society. They may have hoped that the stories they included in their history would shock their readers into seeing how similar their own times were to the times of the judges. They may have hoped that their retelling of the past would lead people in their own time to reexamine their lifestyles and their faith assumptions.

In a similar way, the stark and unpleasant realities pictured in the text of Judges should prompt modern-day readers to ask, "Is history repeating itself in my lifetime? And if so, what can I do about it?" The honesty of the text should encourage readers to consider the causes of violence and terror in their own times as well as in ancient times.

Most of us do not live in a society governed by a king. But even in biblical times, the term *king* often had figurative rather than literal meanings. In biblical texts *kingship* refers to whatever higher authority is acknowledged in people's daily lives. The kingship of the LORD is a central theme in both Old and New Testament texts.

In the religion of Israel, the faithful say the "the LORD is king," meaning that the LORD's authority is supreme among them. In Christian communities, the term *kingdom of God* has the same meaning. When we pray "Thy kingdom come, thy will be done," we are not asking for two things but for one. The coming of the kingdom of God and the doing of the will of God are two halves of the same whole.

Longing for an Ideal King

Human kings in Israel were supposed to uphold and promote the doing of the will of God in the land. The ideal king envisioned by Moses and the prophets would "fear" the LORD and use the covenant to guide the nation in doing what was right in the sight of the LORD (Deuteronomy 17:14-20).

In the absence of a king, the religious authorities might have been expected to provide the Israelites with leadership and instruction in the ways of the LORD. The Levitical priests had been chosen by God "to stand and minister in the name of the LORD" (Deuteronomy 18:5). The Levites had been given special cities of their own within each of the tribal territories, in return for their priestly services. But in the concluding chapters of Judges, even the Levites violate the most basic provisions of the covenant.

Judges 17 introduces us to a man named Micah, who lives in the remote hill country of Ephraim. Micah is clearly in desperate need of spiritual and moral guidance. Like many of our contemporaries, Micah violates a number of commandments in an attempt to find prosperity and security for himself. He sets up his own place of worship, complete with all the trappings of a Canaanite religion.

When an official priest of Israel, "a Levite of Bethlehem in Judah," arrives on the scene, Micah hires him to tend his idolatrous shrine. The Levite, who should have instructed Micah in the laws of the LORD, makes no attempt to sway Micah away from doing "what was right in his own eyes" (17:6).

> When neither the people of God nor their religious and political leaders acknowledge the authority of God, then the least powerful in the land are in danger of being victimized and brutalized.

Instead, this member of the religious establishment lived comfortably off Micah's bounty until he received a more lucrative offer from the thieving tribe of Dan (Judges 18:19-20).

When neither the people of God nor their religious and political leaders acknowledge the authority of God, then the least powerful in the land are in danger of being victimized and brutalized. In Judges 19–21, women are stolen, raped, murdered, and dismembered. They are used to protect men from the aggression of other men. They are forced to marry men who have kidnapped them and men who have murdered their families and friends. But neither God nor our ancestors in the faith approved of such behavior.

When the LORD Is Not Supreme

The violence against women portrayed in Judges 19–21 is a kind of "worst case scenario" in the history of Israel. It is a negative example of the evil that can happen when the LORD does not reign supreme in Israel.

As Christians, we accept the history of Israel as our own history. Through baptism this story becomes the story of our own past. Our ancestors in the faith used these "texts of terror" to warn their own contemporaries that the people of God could easily become like Sodom in the eyes of the LORD. The historians deliberately emphasized the similarities between the outrage at Gibeah and the story of Sodom in Genesis 19, in order to make the point that this lawless village within Israel was no better than the city God had destroyed in Abraham's time. Now we use the same texts to remind ourselves that whenever and wherever the provisions of the covenant are forgotten, the people of God will become as ripe for destruction as Sodom ever was.

Dimension 4:
A Daily Bible Journey Plan

Day 1: Judges 18:1-10

Day 2: Judges 18:11-20

Day 3: Judges 18:21-31

Day 4: Judges 19:1-9

Day 5: Judges 19:10-21

Day 6: Judges 19:22-30

Day 7: Judges 20:1-11

LOVING-KINDNESS TRANSFORMS

What to Watch For

The people of God can and often do choose to pursue a course of action that leads to division and death (as we saw in the final chapters of Judges). But loving-kindness can transform even the darkest hours into occasions for hope. We will see how the Book of Ruth demonstrates what it means to choose loyalty and faithfulness as a way of life.

We will realize that Ruth is not an Israelite. Nevertheless, her actions will reflect the faithfulness and the loving-kindness of Israel's God. Like Rahab (in Joshua 2), Ruth is a foreigner who will choose to align herself with Israel and with Israel's God. Both Ruth and Rahab put their futures in the hand of the LORD. And both Ruth and Rahab will be remembered for the parts they played in the ancestry of the Messiah.

You will notice that the story of Ruth is full of reversals. The action will move from famine to plenty, from emptiness to fullness, from death to new life. And each reversal will begin with an act of loving-kindness.

Read Ruth 1–2 and 4:13-22 to introduce the story.

1. Why did Naomi's family leave Bethlehem, and what prompted Naomi to return when she did? (Ruth 1:1-6)

2. Who does Naomi say is to blame for the bitterness of her situation? (Ruth 1:20-21)

3. What does Ruth give up when she vows to stay with Naomi? (Ruth 1:8-15)

4. What is Ruth doing when she first meets Boaz, and how does Boaz act toward her? (Ruth 2:1-16)

Dimension 2:
What Does the Bible Mean?

The Book of Judges was full of bad news about Israel's disloyalty to God. The Book of Ruth concentrates on some good things that came to pass in the same period of Israel's history. Ruth's story begins with famine and death "in the days when the judges ruled." The story will end with a harvest and a birth that leads to the origin of the messianic line of kings. Ruth and Boaz will become the great-grandparents of David, and David is the key person in Matthew's genealogy of Jesus.

Hesed and the Nature of God

The Book of Ruth revolves around the concept of *hesed* (a Hebrew term meaning "loyalty and loving-kindness"). *Hesed* is an active concept. It is not just an attitude but the enduring and reliable acts of loving-kindness that emerge from that attitude. *Hesed* is not a legal term. One who does *hesed* goes beyond the requirements of the law, beyond the obligations or expectations of society. To do (or to show) *hesed* is to demonstrate goodness or kindness beyond what is expected or deserved by the recipient.

In the Old Testament, *hesed* is considered an essential part of the nature of God. The word is most frequently used to describe the gracious and merciful practices of God. But human beings are also able to do or to show *hesed* to one another. In the Book of Ruth, it is a non-Israelite woman who acts as an agent of God's *hesed* when she herself shows *hesed* to Naomi.

Naomi thinks she has been abandoned or rejected by God. When she urges her daughters-in-law to return to their mothers' homes, she says, "The hand of the LORD has turned against me" (1:13). When she has returned home, she tells the women of Bethlehem, "the Almighty has dealt bitterly with me. . . . The LORD has dealt harshly with me" (1:20-21).

As a widow, Ruth was neither legally nor morally obligated to accompany Naomi back to Bethlehem. No one would have condemned her if she had returned to her own mother's house, as her sister-in-law Orpah did. She was neither obliged nor expected to become her mother-in-law's source of support. But once they are back in Bethlehem she is the one who goes out into the fields to glean the bits of grain that the harvesters missed.

> By committing herself and her future to the LORD, Ruth becomes the means through which God will transform Naomi's emptiness into fulfillment.

Thus, Ruth's speech in 1:16-17 constitutes an act of *hesed*. By committing herself and her future to the LORD, Ruth becomes the means through which God will transform Naomi's emptiness into fulfillment. The LORD will be able to work through the loving-kindness of Ruth to change a crisis situation into an occasion for hope.

Although the action in the Book of Ruth is set in the period of the judges, the final form of the story probably took shape in the postexilic period. When the people of God were freed from their Exile in Babylon sometime after 538 B.C., they returned to Jerusalem and began to rebuild the city and the Temple. One of the greatest problems they faced was the task of restructuring their political and religious life anew. How might the new people of Israel best avoid falling into the snares of idolatry that had lured them away from the LORD from the time of the judges on?

There were basically two schools of thought. Ezra and Nehemiah represented the group that wanted all foreign influences cast out from the midst of the worshiping community. They wanted those of Israelite descent to separate themselves from all foreigners (Nehemiah 13:1-3). They required

Israelite men who had married foreign women to send away their foreign wives and their children (see Ezra 9–10). But the prophet who speaks in Isaiah 56:1-8 argued that the LORD wanted the new community of Israel to include "foreigners who join themselves to the LORD" (Isaiah 56:6) and foreigners who "do what is right" in the eyes of the LORD (56:1).

> Unlike the Israelites by birth who have abandoned the LORD in the period of the judges, Ruth is a foreigner by birth who chooses to become a servant of the LORD and to do the things that please the LORD.

The Book of Ruth argues for this latter point of view. Like Rahab in Joshua 2, and Jael in Judges 4–5, Ruth is a foreign woman who chooses to "join herself to the LORD." Unlike the Israelites by birth who have abandoned the LORD in the period of the judges, Ruth is a foreigner by birth who chooses to become a servant of the LORD and to do the things that please the LORD (Isaiah 56:4, 6). In Ezra, foreign women are cast out of the community. In Ruth, a foreign woman not only marries within the community of Israel she also becomes an ancestor of the Davidic line of kings (Ruth 4:13-22).

Names and Their Meanings

Both the geographical settings and the characters in the Book of Ruth have names with allegorical overtones. Each name hints at the role that place or that character will play in the story. Naomi's name is the only one that is actually explained in the text. *Naomi* is a pun on a Hebrew word meaning "sweet" or "pleasant." But Naomi tells the women of Bethlehem that they might as well call her *Mara* (which means "bitter"), since her life has been full of bitterness (Ruth 1:20-21). Naomi's husband is called *Elimelech*, meaning "my God is king." Immediately after the end of the Book of Judges, we find Elimelech's name reminding us that Israel had no king other than the LORD in this historical period.

The sons of Elimelech and Naomi are called "Sickly" (*Mahlon*) and "Weak" (*Chilion*), leading us to expect their early departure from the scene. Orpah's name means "back of the neck," which seems to be a pun on her behavior as she turns her back on Naomi and Ruth and returns to her mother's household. Boaz has a name based on the Hebrew word for "strength." Ruth's name has a number of possible meanings. *Ruth* sounds like the Hebrew words for friendship, willingness, caretaker, shepherdess, and insight.

There is an ironic pun in the first verse of the story based on the place name *Bethlehem*, which means "house of bread" or "house of food" in Hebrew. The text says that a famine (a lack of bread) caused Elimelech and his family to leave the house of bread. In Ruth 1:6, we are told that

Naomi decided to return home after the death of her husband and sons, because she had heard that bread was now available in the house of bread.

Who Would Despise David's Great-Grandmother?

This allegorical use of names would have indicated to the earliest audiences (the ones who heard the story told in its original language) that Ruth was told as a parable rather than as a factual history. Like the hero in the parable of the good Samaritan, the hero in the Book of Ruth is a member of a group that many Israelites held in utmost contempt. Not only is Ruth a foreigner, she is a Moabite. The people of Moab were despised and rejected by the Israelites. Moabites were denied admittance to the assembly of the LORD, "even to the tenth generation" (Deuteronomy 23:3-4). For the typical Israelite, a Moabite would have seemed like a scandalous choice for the heroine of any story, let alone a story about the origins of the Davidic line of royalty. But Ruth's identity as a daughter of Moab is essential to the point of the story. The narrator repeatedly mentions her Moabite origins, even when that information does not seem relevant to the action (1:22; 2:2, 21; 4:5, 10). Like the servant of the LORD described in Isaiah 53, the "mother" of the messianic line would have been despised and rejected by the very people who would later benefit from her acts of loyalty and loving-kindness.

More Blight on David's Family Tree

However, the author of the Book of Ruth makes the point that the ancestry of Boaz also includes rejected outsiders. The family tree in Ruth 4:17-22 not only looks forward to the birth of David, it also looks backward to an ancestor known as Perez. We are told that Boaz is descended from Perez, as Ruth is descended from Moab. But the story that lies behind the birth of Perez is almost as scandalous as the story that lies behind the birth of Moab.

In Genesis 19, we are told that Moab, the ancestor of Ruth, was born of an incestuous union between Lot and one of his daughters. In Genesis 38, we are told that Perez, the ancestor of Boaz, was also born of an illicit union (although one that some would call justifiable). Perez is the child of a Canaanite widow named Tamar who tricked the father of her deceased husband into having intercourse with her.

> Faith and loving-kindness qualify people to become servants of the LORD, not the purity of their ancestral lines.

Of course, Perez is a somewhat remote ancestor of Boaz. But Ruth 4:21 adds that Salmon was the father of Boaz. This fact does not seem significant until we look at the genealogy of Jesus in Matthew. When Matthew lists the ancestors of Jesus, he tells us that Rahab was the wife of Salmon and the mother of Boaz (Matthew 1:5). In other words, the genealogy in

Ruth 4:18-22 tells us that both parents of Obed had highly disreputable family trees. Furthermore, the genealogy of Jesus in Matthew specifically calls only three women by name (Tamar in 1:3, Rahab and Ruth in 1:6), implying that these three played significant parts in the ancestry of Jesus. Ruth and Matthew seem to score points for the side expressed in Isaiah 56 over against the exclusiveness of Ezra and Nehemiah. All peoples can contribute to the messianic line. It is faith and loving-kindness that qualify people to become servants of the LORD, not the purity of their ancestral lines.

Dimension 3:
What Does the Bible Mean to Us?

Given the degree to which Moabites were despised in Israel, it is possible that Naomi really does not want her Moabite daughters-in-law to accompany her back to Bethlehem. It is equally possible that Naomi (an Israelite who has spent over ten years in Moab) knows all too well how difficult it is to be a stranger in a strange land. In any case, Naomi spells out the implications of her present circumstances in a harsh but realistic way. She repeatedly urges her daughters-in-law to think of their own futures, which are not bound to hers. Orpah accepts the seemingly good sense of Naomi's arguments, but Ruth does not.

Words of a Faithful Commitment

Early Jewish rabbis used the Ruth story as a model for how conversion to Judaism should take place. They noted that Naomi told Ruth to "turn" or "return" three different times before she finally realized how determined Ruth was to accompany her. Thus the early rabbis said that someone who wanted to convert to Judaism should be turned away three times. The difficulties of living as a Jew were to be spelled out in a realistic way. But if the potential convert still persisted after being discouraged three different times, then he or she could be accepted as a committed Jew.

In modern times, several wedding songs have been based on Ruth's speech to Naomi in 1:16-17. Although the words in the biblical text are spoken by one woman to another, they can be seen as a model for any faithful and committed relationship.

But within the context of the whole biblical story, the Book of Ruth stands out as a parable

> The Book of Ruth stands out as a parable of the nature of God's love. Ruth persisted, offering Naomi love and support, even in the face of Naomi's rejection. In a similar way, God persists in loving us even in the face of our rejection.

of the nature of God's love. The parable says that Ruth persisted, offering Naomi love and support, even in the face of Naomi's rejection. In a similar way, the biblical story tells us that God persists in loving us even in the face of our rejection.

The biblical texts frequently remind us that it is not our faithfulness that causes God to love us. Nevertheless, it is clear that human faithfulness is highly valued by God. The story of Ruth suggests that the effective communication of God's love in the world depends on faithful human behavior.

For Bitterness, an Agent of Change

The storyteller makes Naomi's bitterness clear to the audience. In her grief over the deaths of her husband and sons, Naomi feels that the LORD has dealt harshly with her. "I went away full, but the LORD has brought me back empty" (1:21). As the story proceeds, though, Naomi's grief gives way to hope. Her feelings of emptiness are banished (Ruth 4:14-17). In this process of transformation, Ruth is the agent of change. Ruth's acts of loving-kindness communicate the persistence of God's love to Naomi. The conclusion to the story tells us that Ruth's faithfulness will also be an essential element in the carrying out of God's plan for the world through the lineage of David. When loving-kindness is accepted as a way of life, it is possible for ordinary people, living in ordinary circumstances, to bring about extraordinary results.

Boaz is presented to us as a man of substance and piety. He is "a prominent rich man" (Ruth 2:1), who owns more than one field and has a number of servants working for him. When he first appears on the scene he greets the workers in the field with a pious phrase (2:4). And when he speaks with Ruth he invokes the LORD's blessing on her, saying, "May the LORD reward you for your deeds, and may you have a full reward from the LORD, the God of Israel, under whose wings you have come for refuge!" (2:12).

Ruth's reply in 2:13 ("May I continue to find favor in your sight") reminds Boaz that Ruth and Naomi also need earthly, physical help (which he is in a position to supply).

> When loving-kindness is accepted as a way of life, it is possible for ordinary people, living in ordinary circumstances, to bring about extraordinary results.

The covenant code required landowners to set part of every harvest aside for those who had no other source of food (see Leviticus 19:9-10; 23:22; Deuteronomy 24:19-22). Foreigners, widows, and children without a male parent often had no secure means of survival in Israelite society. They were unprotected and defenseless; they had no access to the legal systems of justice. But care for widows and orphans was considered a sign of faithfulness to God.

Occasional Kindness Does Not Remove Poverty

Boaz applies the law in a generous manner to Ruth. He offers her protection (2:8-9), water to drink, and food to eat at mealtime (2:14). He even provides more grain for her to glean than the law requires (2:15-16). But it is still questionable whether his actions count as *hesed* (acts of loving-kindness beyond what is deserved by the recipient).

After all, Boaz is a close relative of Naomi, and therefore of Ruth. He gives to them out of his plenty, with little sacrifice on his own part. And his actions (as they are described in Ruth 2) serve to fill only the immediate needs of the two widows.

They are grateful for his help. But the fact remains that their essential situation of extreme poverty is not changed. As we will see in the next two chapters of Ruth, Boaz's pious wish that the LORD will give Ruth a "full reward" will only come true when he himself takes action to change the circumstances that give rise to the widows' poverty.

The key characters at the close of the Book of Judges were directly descended from Abraham. Nevertheless, they did "whatever seemed right in their own eyes." But the key character in the Book of Ruth is a Moabite. Nevertheless, she has committed herself to carry out God's loving will in her everyday life. It is clear that not Ruth's ancestry but her faithful behavior commends her to God, to Israel, and to us.

The Book of Ruth and Galatians 3:26-29 agree that it is not our physical ancestry but our faithfulness to God that identifies us as descendants of Abraham and heirs to the promise.

Dimension 4:
A Daily Bible Journey Plan

> *Day 1:* Judges 20:12-23
>
> *Day 2:* Judges 20:24-34
>
> *Day 3:* Judges 20:35-48
>
> *Day 4:* Judges 21:1-14
>
> *Day 5:* Judges 21:15-25
>
> *Day 6:* Ruth 1:1-7
>
> *Day 7:* Ruth 1:8-14

13

*L*OVING-KINDNESS GIVES BIRTH TO THE MESSIANIC LINE

What to Watch For

Read the second half of Ruth (Chapters 3 and 4). Notice the plan of action that Naomi will propose to provide security for Ruth's future. You will see Ruth following her mother-in-law's directions, but adding a few words on her own initiative (3:9). In effect, Ruth asks Boaz to marry her and to provide for Naomi's future as well. The narrator will use ambiguous, perhaps suggestive language to describe an encounter to come between Ruth and Boaz on the threshing floor. But the scene will happen in the dark, and readers will remain in the dark. The narrator will not spell out for us what happened between midnight and morning.

Neither Ruth nor Naomi will speak in the final chapter. Boaz will contact an unnamed next-of-kin, who is more closely related to Naomi than Boaz is. Carefully, Boaz will convince that next-of-kin to give up any claim he might have had to the property that once belonged to Naomi's husband. Through a legal fiction, the child born to Ruth and Boaz will be counted both as Elimelech's heir and as the ancestor of David through Boaz.

Dimension 1: What Does the Bible Say?

1. Where does the last of the dialogues between Ruth and Boaz take place? (Ruth 3:6-15)

2. Why does Boaz call the LORD's blessings down on Ruth in Chapter 3?

3. Compare what Ruth tells Naomi in 3:17 with what Boaz actually says to Ruth earlier in 3:15. What does Ruth add on her own initiative?

4. What do the village women say to Naomi about Obed and about Ruth? (Ruth 4:14-15)

Dimension 2: What Does the Bible Mean?

The second half of the Ruth story is more complicated and more difficult for modern readers to understand than the first half. The original narrator and the original audience were members of the same culture. They spoke the same language, they shared a common pool of knowledge, and they held certain ideas and customs in common. But readers today no longer participate in that shared pool of assumptions.

The storyteller assumes that the audience will know what Boaz would be expected to do in his role as a next-of-kin. But we have lost touch with the customs and expectations of Ruth's time. We can only try to reconstruct what these ideas and customs might have been, based on clues we find elsewhere in biblical and in other texts.

Customs Far Removed From Our Day

The action in Chapters 3 and 4 revolves around two customary forms of behavior that seem extremely foreign to our ways of thinking. The first of these customs is referred to as "levirate marriage." Deuteronomy 25:5-6 says that the brother of a dead man is obligated to marry his brother's widow if she has no children. Their firstborn son is to be considered the child of the deceased brother "so that his name may not be blotted out of Israel." This custom of levirate marriage was commonly practiced in a number of ancient Near Eastern societies. It was a way of providing support and protection for widows and an unbroken line for the inheritance of land. Although the law in Deuteronomy says nothing about property rights, we can assume that in Israel, as in other nations, the first child born of a levirate marriage became the deceased man's legal heir.

> We have lost touch with the customs and expectations of Ruth's time. We can only try to reconstruct what these ideas and customs might have been.

The second custom that seems to lie behind the scenes of the action in the second half of Ruth has to do with the redemption of people or property by the next-of-kin. The phrase translated *act as next-of-kin* can also be translated "to redeem." The next-of-kin was the one who was required by law and by custom to redeem persons or property that had been stolen or sold away from the immediate family (see Leviticus 25:25-28; 25:47-54; Jeremiah 32:6-8). It was the duty or obligation of the next-of-kin to buy property that was in danger of being lost to the family (by being sold outside of the family). If the owner was forced to sell in order to survive, the next-of-kin was entitled to first refusal.

These customs both lurk in the background of the negotiations between Ruth and Boaz, as well as the negotiations between Boaz and Naomi's nearer kinsman. But neither of these customs, as they are explained by the legal texts of Israel, seem to fit precisely into the circumstances described in the Book of Ruth.

Did Boaz Feel No Further Obligation?

As Chapter 2 ended, Naomi was rejoicing over the amount of attention Boaz seemed to have showered on Ruth. Boaz had seemed to take such a great interest in Ruth at the beginning of the grain harvest season. Naomi had begun to hope that Boaz would do something to change the unprotected and vulnerable circumstances in which the two widows lived. But as the harvest season (which is at least seven weeks long) progressed, Boaz apparently felt he had done enough. He seems to have taken no further action on behalf of either Ruth or Naomi.

When Chapter 3 opens, we find that Naomi has decided that it is time for the women to take matters into their own hands. Naomi feels that Boaz needs to be prodded (or should we say trapped?) into making a further commitment to Ruth. The text says that Naomi justifies her plan as an attempt to find some lasting security for Ruth (3:1-4).

Ruth follows Naomi's directions. After she has bathed, perfumed, and dressed in her best clothes, she slips onto the threshing floor where Boaz is sleeping. She uncovers the lower half of his body and lies down beside him. The word translated *feet* in 3:4 and 3:7-8 actually refers to the legs or to the lower half of the body. Sometimes it is a euphemism for the genitals. There is no way to know what the narrator intended for the audience to think on this occasion. The language permits any of these possibilities.

Naomi thought Boaz would tell Ruth "what to do" when he found her lying next to him (3:4). But Ruth does not wait to be told. She takes the initiative and asks Boaz to "spread his cloak [wings] over" her (3:9). In other words, she asks Boaz to take her under his wing or under his protection. Ruth uses the same phrase here in 3:9 to refer to Boaz's protection as Boaz had used in an earlier conversation (2:12) to refer to the LORD's protection. The same word can be translated as either "wing" or "cloak."

Thus Ruth does what Naomi tells her to do to guarantee her own security. But she also takes steps to provide for Naomi's future. Ruth reminds Boaz that he is one of those who have the right to redeem Naomi's husband's property (3:9). Boaz agrees to do everything Ruth asks him to do (3:11). But there is one problem: Boaz knows that there is another kinsman who is more closely related to Naomi than he is. Chapter 4 tells us how Boaz manages to overcome this potential complication.

Inside the City Gate

In this story, where almost all of the characters' names have symbolic value, the next-of-kin is never referred to by name. (In 4:1, "Come over, friend" might better be translated as either "So-and-So" or "What's-His-Name.") This is a clue that his identity is insignificant in the story. Boaz sets up the conditions for a public hearing, which traditionally would take place just inside the city gates. In the presence of ten respected citizens ("elders") who will serve as witnesses, he officially informs So-and-So that Naomi is selling the parcel of land that belonged to their kinsman Elimelech. Everyone would have known that So-and-So had the right of first refusal to buy the property. But when it seemed that So-and-So was inclined to redeem the property, thus increasing his own land holdings, Boaz was ready to add another bit of information (in 4:5).

There is, however, some difficulty in understanding what the original Hebrew in 4:5 actually said. The statement can be understood in two possible ways. The NRSV makes it sound like So-and-So will be expected to father a child for Ruth if he redeems the land. If this is the case, then the custom on which this expectation is based is unknown to us. The levirate marriage law has to do with brothers in the same household (Deuteronomy 25:7-10).

But the original text can also be understood in a different way. The translation of 4:5 could possibly read, "The day you acquire the field from the hand of Naomi, I [Boaz] will acquire Ruth, the Moabite, the widow of the dead man, to maintain the dead man's name on his inheritance." In other words, Boaz declares his intention to marry Ruth and to designate their first son the heir of Ruth's dead husband. In effect, Boaz says, "You have the right of first refusal to buy the land, but you should know that I plan to marry Ruth and declare our first son heir to Elimelech. Our first child will carry on Elimelech's family name. He will be able to claim back the property that you propose to buy."

What Boaz plans to do is not precisely the same as the levirate marriage spelled out in Deuteronomy 25. But Boaz uses similar language. He says that his purpose is "to maintain the dead man's name on his inheritance" (4:5, 10). Ruth's first child will be regarded (by a legal fiction) as the child of Ruth's deceased husband, Mahlon. In the end, however, the genealogy counts Obed as the son of Boaz, not as a descendant of Mahlon or Elimelech. Property claims aside, the line leading to the birth of David runs through Boaz.

An Heir Through Loving-kindness

When Boaz simply gave Ruth extra grain to take home to Naomi, he was not performing an act of *hesed*. But redeeming and restoring the heritage of Ruth's first husband's family would certainly qualify as an act of loyalty and loving-kindness. Boaz had no legal obligations in this case. It is an act of *hesed* for him to reestablish Elimelech's heritage. Thus the line of the Messiah arises, not from the doing of covenantal obligations, but from the doing of deeds of loving-kindness on the parts of both Ruth and Boaz.

The historians blamed the violence described in the Book of Judges on the lack of God-fearing leadership in Israel (Judges 21:25). They knew that Israel needed a king. They also knew that not just any king would do.

> The historians blamed the violence described in Judges on the lack of God-fearing leadership in Israel. They knew that Israel needed a king. They also knew that not just any king would do.

In the biblical books that follow Judges and Ruth, we will see that the people's first attempt to choose a king for themselves was destined to fail. Saul was a Benjaminite, of Gibeah (1 Samuel 10:26). Thus his kingship was symbolically rooted in the same place and in the same self-centered attitude that characterized the sin and violence described in Judges 19–21.

The house of David
had its foundations in
loving relationships
between the powerless
and the powerful,
between native born
and foreigners.

But the historians say that the Davidic line of kings had God-fearing origins. God had promised David, "I will raise up your offspring after you. . . . I will establish the throne of his kingdom forever. . . . I will not take my steadfast love from him, as I took it from Saul" (2 Samuel 7:12-13, 15).

The house of David had its foundations in loving relationships between the powerless and the powerful, between native born and foreigners.

Dimension 3:
What Does the Bible Mean to Us?

The Book of Ruth contains subversive literature. The term *subversive* implies an attempt to undermine or to overturn the usual standards of behavior or judgment that prevailed in a society. Israel had a very strict standard of behavior with regard to Moabites. Ruth turns that standard upside down. Ezra and Nehemiah promoted prejudice in Israel against foreign wives. Ruth turns that prejudice on its head. And, finally, Ruth undermines the male Israelite belief that God favors submissive, nonaggressive behavior on the part of women.

Subversive and Scandalous
The course of actions proposed by Naomi (3:1-5) and followed by Ruth would have been considered scandalous according to the moral norms of Israelite society. The narrator makes it clear that Boaz wanted to keep his threshing-floor encounter with Ruth out of the public eye. Boaz says to himself, "It must not be known that the woman came to the threshing floor" (3:14). And yet, the genealogy at the end of the story forces the reader to acknowledge that this socially unacceptable behavior will eventually lead to the birth of the Messiah.

This point is reinforced by the blessings that the townspeople pronounce on Boaz (4:11-12). The people of Bethlehem connect or equate Ruth with three women in Israel's past: Rachel, Leah, and Tamar. The narrator naturally expects the audience to know all of the stories associated with the women named in the blessings.

What do the stories connected with these women have in common with Ruth's story? Each woman mentioned in the blessings had participated in the "building up of the house of Israel." But each of them did so in subversive ways. Leah uttered not a word all night long to tip off Jacob that he was spending his wedding night with the sister of his beloved (Genesis

29:23). Rachel, her sister, soon became Jacob's wife, too. Unable to conceive, Rachel manipulated her husband's activity so that Jacob fathered ten sons. Then "God remembered Rachel, and God heeded her and opened her womb" (Genesis 30:22). At last she gave birth—to Joseph. Tamar, when widowed, was not given in a levirate marriage to her husband's surviving brother by her father-in-law, Judah. So, she used the subterfuge of appearing to be a prostitute to get Judah to father a child for her (Genesis 38).

Each story involves a deception played by women on men who were supposedly in control of their reproductive futures. In each story the traditional role of the male in Israelite society is overruled by female initiative. (We find in Ruth 4:13 and Genesis 30:17 and 30:22 that God is given credit for the conception of these mothers of the promise.)

The blessings pronounced by the people of Bethlehem also remind us that the firstborn is the one society expects to inherit. Who actually does inherit in these subversive situations? Perez, like other heirs of the promise in Genesis, was the younger in the line of inheritance. Mahlon was the younger of Naomi's two sons, and Boaz was younger than So-and-So. It seems clear that God does not choose agents of redemption according to human standards or according to the expectations of society.

Ruth's initial acts of *hesed* help to change Naomi's attitude from bitterness to hope. Together the two women help to change Boaz from one who merely gave charity from his bounty to one who provided a solution for the problem that had impoverished these women.

Words and Deeds

There is an interplay in this story between the things people say and the things they do. Boaz speaks in a pious and gracious manner, as we might expect a respected member of the community to do. But in spite of his apparent sincerity, Boaz has to be maneuvered (or at least nudged) into rescuing his close relatives from their impoverished circumstances. It seems that Boaz is attracted to Ruth from the time they first meet. It seems he is flattered by the fact that Ruth has chosen to come to him rather than going to one of the younger men on the threshing floor (3:10). So why did he need to be pushed into making Ruth an offer?

> The characters speak about God. They invoke God's blessings. But it is human beings who personify and communicate the loving-kindness of God in the world.

Did the fact that there was a nearer kinsman justify Boaz's inaction? Wouldn't a truly god-fearing person have prodded So-and-So into doing what needed to be done? Perhaps Boaz has an overly high regard for public opinion. In 4:14, he seems concerned for his own reputation as well as for Ruth's standing in the community. He may have been reluctant to go against the standards of his own community by offering marriage to a Moabite. But when Ruth speaks in the dark on the threshing floor, she challenges Boaz to put his pious words into action. In effect, she says, "Make your words about the shelter of God's wing come true by taking me under the shelter of your wing."

Although Ruth seems to be the heroine of the story that bears her name, she actually speaks less (and in a less-revealing manner) in the story than either Naomi or Boaz. We are not told what motivates Ruth's behavior or what she thought about the other characters' actions. What we think or know about Ruth comes primarily from the comments the other characters in the story make to her or about her.

When Naomi told the women of Bethlehem that the LORD had brought her back empty, she evidently did not consider the loyal and loving presence of her daughter-in-law worth mentioning. In the end, however, the women of Bethlehem have the last word about Ruth's value. They tell Naomi in no uncertain terms, "Your daughter-in-law who loves you . . . is more to you than seven sons" (4:15).

The grain that Boaz gives to Ruth and Ruth gives to Naomi seems to symbolize their future together. Ruth is the one who makes it possible for Boaz's seed to be counted as Elimelech's seed.

Except for the narrator's statement that the LORD made Ruth conceive (4:13), the narrator does not have God speak or act directly in the story. The characters speak about God. They invoke God's blessings on one another. But it is human beings who personify and communicate the loving-kindness of God in the world. Everything the LORD gives in this story (including the conception of the child) comes through human interaction. God's love embodied in humankind gives birth to the messianic line.

Dimension 4:
A Daily Bible Journey Plan

Day 1: **Ruth 1:15-22**

Day 2: **Ruth 2:1-13**

Day 3: **Ruth 2:14-23**

Day 4: **Ruth 3:1-13**

Day 5: **Ruth 3:14—4:6**

Day 6: **Ruth 4:7-12**

Day 7: **Ruth 4:13-22**

GLOSSARY

Achan (AY-kan)—an Israelite who helped himself to objects "devoted to God" (Joshua 7:1-26)

Achsah (AK-suh)—daughter of Caleb (one of twelve spies sent by Moses into Promised Land); she asked for and received a present of land in her own name (Joshua 15:16-19)

Barak (BAIR-ak)—of the tribe of Naphtali; following advice of Deborah led ten thousand Israelite warriors against Sisera, general of a Canaanite army (Judges 4:6-16)

Boaz (BO-azz)—a prosperous farmer of Bethlehem who married the Moabite, Ruth (Ruth 2:1)

Canaan (KAY-nuhn)—the Promised Land; the land promised by God to Abraham and his descendants forever (Genesis 12:1-7); the land into which Joshua led the Israelites (Joshua 1:1-6)

Canon (KAN-unh)—originally meant "straight rod"; came to mean those writings accepted as Scripture and used as a rule of faith and practice

Deborah (DEB-uh-ruh)—a prophetess and judge; told Barak to lead Israelite troops against Canaanite forces led by Sisera; composed a victory song after the victory (Judges 4; 5)

Ehud (EE-huhd)—a judge; a "left-handed man"; led the Israelites against Moab; killed the Moabite king by a subterfuge (Judges 3:12-30)

Gideon (GID-ee-unh)—a judge of Israel; led small army with which God defeated the Midianites (Judges 6–8)

Jael (JAY-uhl)—wife of Heber the Kenite; killed Sisera when he came to her tent to escape Barak (Judges 4:17-22)

Jephthah (JEF-thuh)—a judge of Israel; led Israelites to victory over Ammonites; made vow to the LORD for victory; vow resulted in death of his daughter (Judges 11)

Jericho (JER-ur-koh)—city in the valley of the Jordan, near northern end of Dead Sea; first city to fall to Israelites during the conquest (Joshua 6)

111

Jordan (JOR-duhn)—most important river in Palestine; crossed by Israelites under Joshua to enter the Promised Land (Joshua 3)

Joshua (JOSH-yoo-uh)—"Son of Nun"; leader of the Israelites after Moses' death (Joshua 1:1-2)

Naomi (nay-OH-mee)—wife of Elimelech; mother-in-law of Ruth, a Moabite; both were widowed in Moab and traveled to Bethelehem, Naomi's home; arranged Ruth's marriage to Boaz; considered grandmother to Obed (Ruth 1–4)

Nazirite (NAZ-uh-rite)—person specially consecrated to God (Numbers 6:1-21); Samson was a nazirite (Judges 13)

Obed (OH-bid)—son of Ruth and Boaz; David's grandfather (Ruth 4:13-17)

Othniel (OTH-nee-uhl)—a judge of Israel; won Achsah, daughter of Caleb, as his wife; defeated the king of Aram (Judges 1:12-13; 2:7-11)

Rahab (RAY-hab)—a prostitute who lived in Jericho; helped the Israelites who were sent to spy out Jericho; she and her family were spared because of her help (Joshua 2:1-21; 6:22-23)

Ruth (rooth)—Moabite woman, widow of Mahlon, daughter-in-law of Naomi; traveled with Naomi to Bethlehem; met and married Boaz and became mother of Obed, grandfather of David (Book of Ruth)

Samson (SAM-suhn)—a judge of Israel and a nazirite from birth; known for his strength; captured by Philistines when Delilah learned his secret and cut his hair, breaking his nazirite vow (Judges 13–16)

Shechem (SHEK-uhm)—the place where God first promised that the land of Canaan would be home to Abraham's offspring (Genesis 12:6-7); Joshua challenged the people to renew their covenant with the LORD (Joshua 24)

Sisera (SIS-uh-ruh)—general of Canaanite king Jabin's army; was routed by Barak and killed by Jael (Judges 4:7; 12-22; 5:18-21, 24-27)

Zelophehad (zuh-LOH-fud-had)—father of five daughters (Mahlah, Noah, Hoglah, Milcah, Tirzah), no sons; daughters petitioned for their right to inherit "along with our male kin" (Joshua 17:3)

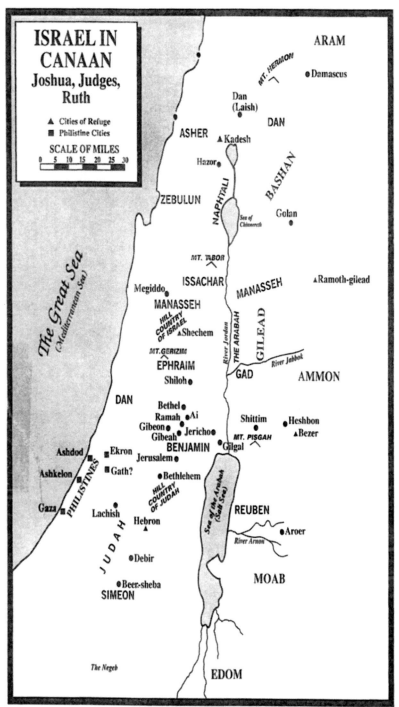

ISRAEL IN CANAAN
Joshua, Judges, Ruth

▲ Cities of Refuge
■ Philistine Cities

SCALE OF MILES
0 5 10 15 20 25 30

ARAM

● Damascus

MT. HERMON

Dan
(Laish)

DAN

ASHER   ▲ Kadesh

Hazor ●

BASHAN

NAPHTALI

ZEBULUN

Sea of
Chinnereth

● Golan

MT. TABOR

ISSACHAR

MANASSEH

▲ Ramoth-gilead

Megiddo ●

MANASSEH

HILL
COUNTRY
OF ISRAEL   ▲ Shechem

GILEAD

River Jordan

THE ARABAH

River Jabbok

MT. GERIZIM

EPHRAIM

Shiloh ●

GAD

AMMON

The Great Sea
(Mediterranean Sea)

DAN

Bethel ●
Ramah ● ● Ai
Gibeon ●
Gibeah ● ● Jericho

Shittim ●

● Heshbon
▲ Bezer

MT. PISGAH

BENJAMIN   ● Gilgal

Ashdod
■ Ekron
Jerusalem ●
Ashkelon
■ Gath?

PHILISTINES

● Bethlehem

HILL
COUNTRY
OF JUDAH

Sea of the Arabah
(Salt Sea)

Gaza ■

Lachish ●

Hebron ●
▲

J U D A H

REUBEN

● Aroer

River Arnon

● Debir

● Beer-sheba

SIMEON

MOAB

The Negeb

EDOM

Adapted from *Bible Teacher Kit* © by Abingdon Press, 1994.

.

CPSIA information can be obtained at www.ICGtesting.com
Printed in the USA
BVOW012044300513

322058BV00009B/167/P